What Would Happen?

CRISPIN BOYER

NATIONAL GEOGRAPHIC
KiDS

WASHINGTON, D.C.

What Would Happen?

Contents

Reality Checked!

"What's done is done."
"You **can't always get** what you want."
"That's the way the cookie **crumbles."**

These words are wise in the real world, where history is already written, technology has its limitations, and the laws of physics keep everyone from leaping tall buildings in a single bound. But what if you could redo the past? What if you could reinvent yourself with wings or gills or astounding superpowers? What if you could ask "what if?" and see the answer play out before your eyes?

Welcome to *What Would Happen?*, the book that gives you a new look at everything: past and present, space and time, people and places, wildlife and a life that's wild. You'll find nearly a hundred scenarios across a variety of topics, from a new spin on Earth to historic do-overs to mind-blowing situations that defy physics.

Each scenario has been exhaustively researched and assembled with feedback from experts, turning *What Would Happen?* into more than just a book—it's a vacation from the real world! By the time you've wandered through all the wonders of this book, you'll know what would have happened if the dinosaurs survived, what would happen if all mosquitoes died, and how the government would react if zombies attacked. Some scenarios are inspired by sci-fi. (Buckle up for an elevator ride to space!) Some are serious. (Don't panic if your parachute fails!) And some are pretty silly. (Turns out a junk-food diet might have you craving broccoli.) But, hey—that's the way the cookie crumbles.

Feeling Iffy

Packed with facts and overflowing with info, each page of *What Would Happen?* is like a portal to an alternate reality. Here's how to see it all ...

Know Before You Go!

Before you dive into each scenario, dip your toes here for the details behind the story.

Big Changes Are Afoot!

Here you'll find the scenario's primary repercussions: how life would be different in a world where your what-if question came true.

What if

an asteroid hadn't wiped out the dinosaurs?

The world would be a different place—and you wouldn't be around to see it.

Tyrannosaurus rex never saw it coming. Around 66 million years ago, an asteroid or comet nearly the size of San Francisco slammed into the seabed off the Yucatán Peninsula in Mexico at 45,000 miles an hour (72,420 km/h). Shock waves and tsunamis as tall as skyscrapers scoured nearby landmasses of all trees and dirt down to the bedrock, while the impact hurtled dust and vapor to the edge of Earth's atmosphere. Then things got really bad. A global heat wave was followed by a planetwide chill. Over the next few thousand years, roughly 75 percent of all species went extinct, including most of the dinosaurs. But what if that direct hit had been a miss?

END OF THEIR WORLD

You Who?

The dino-doomsday left a void for smarter, smaller animals to fill. Among them were the mammals. These furry creatures had scurried beneath the feet of dinosaurs for nearly 150 million years, scavenging for scraps while running for their lives. Suddenly the world was all theirs. Mammals took advantage of the situation by growing in size and diversifying into many of the species we know today: cats, dogs, horses, bats, and primates—the order of animals that eventually gave rise to gorillas, chimpanzees, and *Homo sapiens* (aka, the human species).

But if that asteroid had sailed past Earth, "there's no reason to think dinosaurs would have died out," says Stephen Brusatte, a paleontologist at the University of Edinburgh in Scotland. "They had been around for 160 million years and were doing fine. And without dinosaurs dying out, mammals would have never gotten their chance, and our ancestors wouldn't have evolved." In other words, you, your pooch, and everyone you know today owe their existence to a cosmic accident.

54

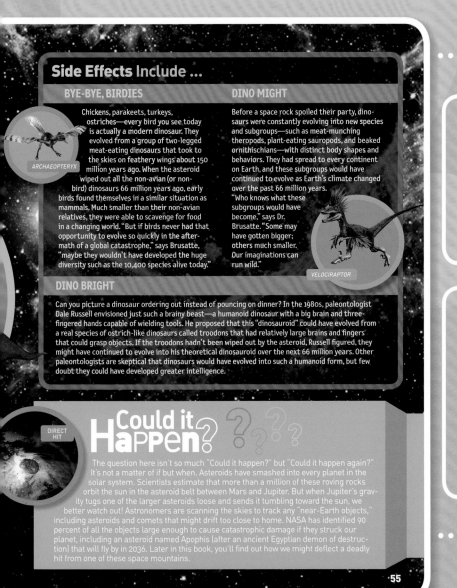

Side Effects Include ...

BYE-BYE, BIRDIES

Chickens, parakeets, turkeys, ostriches—every bird you see today is actually a modern dinosaur. They evolved from a group of two-legged meat-eating dinosaurs that took to the skies on feathery wings about 150 million years ago. When the asteroid wiped out all the non-avian (or non-bird) dinosaurs 66 million years ago, early birds found themselves in a similar situation as mammals. Much smaller than their non-avian relatives, they were able to scavenge for food in a changing world. "But if birds never had that opportunity to evolve so quickly in the aftermath of a global catastrophe," says Brusatte, "maybe they wouldn't have developed the huge diversity such as the 10,400 species alive today."

ARCHAEOPTERYX

DINO MIGHT

Before a space rock spoiled their party, dinosaurs were constantly evolving into new species and subgroups—such as meat-munching theropods, plant-eating sauropods, and beaked ornithischians—with distinct body shapes and behaviors. They had spread to every continent on Earth, and these subgroups would have continued to evolve as Earth's climate changed over the past 66 million years. "Who knows what these subgroups would have become," says Dr. Brusatte. "Some may have gotten bigger; others much smaller. Our imaginations can run wild."

VELOCIRAPTOR

DINO BRIGHT

Can you picture a dinosaur ordering out instead of pouncing on dinner? In the 1980s, paleontologist Dale Russell envisioned just such a brainy beast—a humanoid dinosaur with a big brain and three-fingered hands capable of wielding tools. He proposed that this "dinosauroid" could have evolved from a real species of ostrich-like dinosaurs called troodons that had relatively large brains and fingers that could grasp objects. If the troodons hadn't been wiped out by the asteroid, Russell figured, they might have continued to evolve into his theoretical dinosauroid over the next 66 million years. Other paleontologists are skeptical that dinosaurs would have evolved into such a humanoid form, but few doubt they could have developed greater intelligence.

Could it Happen❓

DIRECT HIT

The question here isn't so much "Could it happen?" but "Could it happen again?" It's not a matter of if but when. Asteroids have smashed into every planet in the solar system. Scientists estimate that more than a million of these roving rocks orbit the sun in the asteroid belt between Mars and Jupiter. But when Jupiter's gravity tugs one of the larger asteroids loose and sends it tumbling toward the sun, we better watch out! Astronomers are scanning the skies to track any "near-Earth objects," including asteroids and comets that might drift too close to home. NASA has identified 90 percent of all the objects large enough to cause catastrophic damage if they struck our planet, including an asteroid named Apophis (after an ancient Egyptian demon of destruction) that will fly by in 2036. Later in this book, you'll find out how we might deflect a deadly hit from one of these space mountains.

·55·

Side Effects Include ...

Not every change will rock your world. Here you'll find the smaller, often stranger consequences resulting from your what-if question.

Could It Happen?

Here you'll find the chances that these changes might actually come to pass. Consider this section good news or bad news—depending on whether you thought the scenario was a dream or a nightmare.

Got the gist? Good! Now turn the page. You're ready for what-if liftoff!

Chapter 1

You First

You can sing. You can boogie. You can ponder the mysteries of the universe or cram a big ball of cookie dough in your mouth. From the top of your brain's frontal lobes to the tips of your big toes, you are an amazing biological machine capable of outrageously cool things. But what if you could add flight to your list of abilities? Or superstrength? What if you never stopped growing? Or never started bathing? Prepare to ponder powers and situations that range from super-duper to super-silly in this chapter that introduces you to the yous from alternate realities.

What if you had wings like a bird?

What Would Happen if...

What if you ate nothing but ice cream?

I scream, you scream, we all scream for ... fiber and protein?

Butter pecan for breakfast. Rocky road for lunch. Mint chocolate chip for dinner. And for dessert? More ice cream, of course! Frosty sweets for every meal, every day might sound like a miracle menu. (Bye-bye, Brussels sprouts! Cookies and cream instead of creamed spinach!) But the consequences of slurping down all that frozen milk fat would be sour rather than sweet. Open wide for the disappointing truth in this sweet tooth's dream turned nightmare ...

Highly Irregular

Ice cream is a simple thing, made mainly of milk, cream (fat skimmed off the top of milk), sugar, and flavor (chocolate, vanilla, strawberry, etc.). As far as junk foods go, you could stuff worse things into your belly. Ice cream has calcium for strong bones, a little protein for your muscles, and a few vitamins. But it lacks one substance that your body will miss in a matter of days: dietary fiber. Also known as roughage, fiber is the indigestible stuff in fruits, veggies, and grains.

If your body can't digest fiber, why is it so important? In the long term, roughage helps prevent heart disease, diabetes, and other illnesses. In the short term, it keeps you on, shall we say, a regular schedule. "If you go several days without eating fiber,

you would get terribly constipated," says nutritionist Jo Ann Hattner, registered dietician and author of the book *Gut Insight*. Roughage is like grease in the gears of your guts. It keeps food moving along and helps your body extract nutrients at each step in the digestive tract, right up to the exit. Snack on roughage-free foods such as ice cream for too long and you'll do a lot of sitting in the bathroom, waiting for something to happen. Your number-one solution for going number two is to think outside the bowl. "You could solve this problem if you topped your ice cream with broccoli," Hattner says, "but that kind of defeats the purpose."

Side Effects Include ...

POWER DOWN

Like all dairy products, ice cream contains some protein but not enough for your body's needs. A lack of protein in your diet not only saps your strength—it can be dangerous! "Protein is what rebuilds your muscles after you use them," Hattner says. "If you only eat ice cream, you're not replacing any of your muscle mass." You would begin to feel weak and tired all the time. Muscles would start to wither and ache. Things would only get worse until you started snacking on more protein-rich foods.

C MINUS

Until nearly the end of the 18th century, sailors living at sea for months at a time would become feverish and weak from an illness called scurvy. The culprit: a dull diet lacking in vitamin C—a crucial nutritional need that your body doesn't store. It's found in citrus fruits such as oranges and limes, as well as in some vegetables. Ice cream contains only about one percent of your body's daily requirement of vitamin C. Eat it and nothing else for too long, and you'll wind up in the same boat as those ancient mariners.

Could it Happen?

The only way to make an ice-cream diet work is to cheat on it. But unlike most diet cheats, this menu addition is no guilty pleasure. It's all about the toppings! To add roughage to your rocky road, drop on some cauliflower, a few leaves of spinach, and a little granola. For the necessary protein, dump in some nuts and even a few chunks of chicken or tofu. For vitamin C, pile on orange slices and maybe a few tomatoes. By the time you've topped your ice cream with the necessary nutritional supplements, you'll have more of a sugary stew than a frosty treat. If the cavities from all that sugar—not to mention all those agonizing ice-cream headaches—don't drive you to a more balanced diet, your own cravings for other flavors (salt, fat, cheeseburgers, etc.) will. "Humans hate monotony," Hattner says. "We were really meant to eat a variety of food."

What if you had **wings** like a **bird**?

QUETZALCOATLUS

Don't cancel your plane tickets just yet.

People have been taking to the skies for more than 200 years—first in hot-air balloons and later in winged flying machines—but we've been dreaming of leaving the ground for much longer. The ancient Greeks told the legend of Icarus, the daring flyboy who soared too close to the sun on wings made of wax and feathers. In the late 1400s, Italian artist Leonardo da Vinci studied birds to sketch an "ornithopter" flying machine with flapping wings powered by levers and foot pedals. But what if humans had wings all along? Would we soar to school each morning or crash and burn like Icarus? Prepare for one tricky takeoff ...

The **Thing** About **Wings**

To see whether a winged human could even get off the ground, we need to look at the largest animal that ever flew: the *Quetzalcoatlus*. This freaky long-necked pterosaur (or winged reptile) had the wing-span of a fighter plane and a 10-foot (3-m)-long head with a beak that tapered to a sharp point. It soared above lakes and plains about 66 million years ago, at the end of the age of dinosaurs.

The *Quetzalcoatlus* had a body evolved for flight, with hollow bones and powerful wing muscles. Humans, on the other hand, are bound for the ground. Our bones are dense. Our muscles are heavy. Scientists estimate that a human would need a wingspan more

than 22 feet (7 m)—possibly up to 80 feet (24 m)—to create enough lifting force to propel us into the air.

And our need for big wings presents a bigger problem: the need for big muscles to power them. When you add in the weight of these extra muscles, the size of your wings is no longer sufficient to lift you off the ground. You'll need even larger wings to lift these muscles, and then more powerful muscles to lift these wings. You're locked in a never-ending escalation of wingspan and muscle mass. The only way we would get off the ground is if we evolved with hollow bones and lightweight bodies, just like the *Quetzalcoatlus*.

LATE 19TH-CENTURY GLIDER

WINGSUIT

Air Time: What It's Like to Fly ...

Imagine standing at the edge of a cliff, dressed in a nylon zip-up suit that's like footy pajamas with wings stretched between the arms and legs. This ensemble—part superhero outfit, part flying squirrel cosplay—is called a "wingsuit," and it's the closest humans can get to flying with wings and nothing else. Wingsuit skydivers fly forward as they fall and can control their direction, soaring like Superman while skimming mountainsides and dodging terrain until they must deploy a parachute for a safe landing.

Stephanie "Steph" Davis knows what it's like to fly with a wingsuit. This expert climber has also mastered the extreme sport of skydiving from buildings, bridges, and mountains, and now she's going to share the experience with you. Here, Davis describes the sensation of a thrillingly typical wingsuit jump from the edge of a mountaintop cliff ...

"You feel the wind, look out over the landscape below, and think about where you will fly and where you will land. Once you leave the edge, there's no going back. The first seconds are the most important, when you really don't want to mess up. You take a few deep breaths, shake out your wings, and then focus your eyes straight out ahead into the air and push off the edge of the cliff. For a second you're falling into soft air. In the next second, your wings start to inflate with air and get more rigid. You wait for a half second more, open your leg wing, and start to shoot forward instead of diving straight down. You're going 100 miles an hour [161 km/h], and you're screaming forward and moving in three dimensions. But it also seems slow as you watch the world below, tuck your shoulders forward and stretch your legs as hard as you can for maximum speed, turning your body like a fish: left, right, or down. It's flying, and it feels exactly like you always thought it would. You watch the trees go by, the rocks beside you, you see the ground getting closer, and you reach back and throw out the parachute."

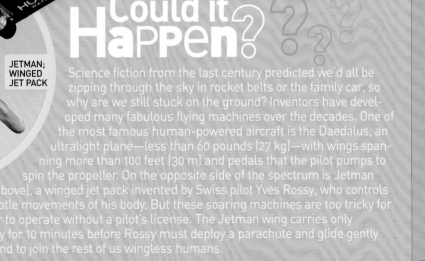

JETMAN; WINGED JET PACK

Could it Happen?

Science fiction from the last century predicted we'd all be zipping through the sky in rocket belts or the family car, so why are we still stuck on the ground? Inventors have developed many fabulous flying machines over the decades. One of the most famous human-powered aircraft is the Daedalus, an ultralight plane—less than 60 pounds [27 kg]—with wings spanning more than 100 feet [30 m] and pedals that the pilot pumps to spin the propeller. On the opposite side of the spectrum is Jetman (above), a winged jet pack invented by Swiss pilot Yves Rossy, who controls his craft with subtle movements of his body. But these soaring machines are too tricky for the average flyer to operate without a pilot's license. The Jetman wing carries only enough fuel to fly for 10 minutes before Rossy must deploy a parachute and glide gently back to the ground to join the rest of us wingless humans.

What if you **never** aged?

Better find a few hobbies. Eternal life could get boring.

No need to rage over aging. It happens to the best of us! That doesn't make growing old any less mysterious—especially to scientists. Healthy humans can heal, recover from illnesses, and replicate their cells again and again, so why can't this process continue forever? Old age and death are hardly beneficial to our species' survival, after all. According to one theory, our life span is programmed into our cells, which initiate the aging process once we're beyond our reproductive years. Another theory holds that our cells have a sort of expiration date and can only reproduce so many times. Scientists are researching ways to press pause on the aging process. What if they succeed?

Life Sentence

Vampire movies make immortality look like a glamorous good time, but the day-to-day reality of eternal life might not get your blood pumping. You'll find your endless days divided into several stages. First up: the grief stage. As the only immortal on a planet of mortals (we're assuming you're alone in this scenario; otherwise, Earth would eventually fill to standing room only), you would see all your friends and family members grow old and die. Next comes boredom. Entertainment options would fail to hold your interest after you've seen every Star Wars movie 50 times or read the Harry Potter series until you're able quote each book from memory. New flicks, novels, and songs might hold your interest for a while, but eventually all the remakes and sequels would start to feel too familiar.

As the decades stretched into centuries and then into millennia, you'd need to quit procrastinating (easy to do when you live forever) and look after your own needs. Want fresh entertainment, you'd better

start writing your own. Learn every language to enrich your life with arts, entertainment, and cool people to chat with. Money wouldn't be a problem (you'd always have a stack of vintage toys to sell online), but a life of leisure would lose its luster. You'd become a jack-of-all-trades—a brain surgeon, fighter pilot, garbage-truck driver, carpenter—with plenty of time to master them all.

But eventually, you'd reach the final stage of immortality: restlessness. After climbing every mountain, eating in every restaurant, beating every video game, and plunging to the depths of every abyss on Earth—hundreds of times—you'll be ready for a change of scenery. If the rocket scientists haven't perfected space travel, you'll begin to devise your own. No rush. You have all the time in the worlds.

The **Ups** and **Downs** of Eternal Youth

Pros

Skill-Building: Unlimited time to master the guitar, become a gourmet chef, learn every language, etc.

Good Looks: Defy wrinkles, gray hairs, lousy eyesight, and other symptoms of your golden years.

Thinking Big: Make your mark on history, then read about your exploits later in the history books.

Cons

Sad Goodbyes: Mourn the losses of loved ones who pass away while you don't age a day.

Bored to Death: Trying everything once will be fun. Trying everything 99 times? Not so much.

Birthday Dangers: Firefighters will become regular birthday guests once your cake tops 1,000 candles.

See next page for more!

Time Out

Time flies not just when you're having fun. Studies show your brain perceives the passage of time more rapidly as you grow older. Why? Two reasons: When you're young, life is full of first-time experiences that turn every day into a new adventure. These experiences become humdrum as they repeat throughout your life. The other reason: When you're young, the majority of your life lies before you and you have relatively fewer years behind you. Think about how your summer vacations unfold. For the first month or so after the final bell rings in June, the rest of summer seems to stretch out forever. But as you near the end of your vacation, each moment of freedom becomes more precious—and therefore seems to pass more quickly. This same principle applies to your immortal life. Eventually, as the centuries fade behind you, years and even decades will seem to pass faster and faster, until new friends flit into your life and grow old practically before your eyes.

Side Effects of Eternal Life Include ...

BRAIN DRAIN

Your brain's capacity to retain memories is vast but not bottomless. By some accounts, your noggin can store about 2,560 terabytes of long-term memories: enough to hold 300 million hours of TV shows. That's plenty of space for one lifetime, but eternity of new memories will eventually clog up your noggin until you're left struggling to recall where you left your jet pack keys.

PROCEED WITH CAUTION

Just because you're immune to aging, diseases, and (presumably) hunger doesn't mean you're indestructible. Careless accidents and daredevil stunts can still land you in the hospital with busted bones and long-term injuries. What's the point of living forever if you're stuck in a full-body cast or lost in some endless network of caves?

> 66 If all age-related causes of death and ill health could be eliminated by medical nanorobotics, then there are only five remaining nonmedical causes of death [all accidental or caused by humans]. If you add up the statistical death rates from all five causes, and if we assume that these are the sole causes of death, then the average disease-free life span would be about 1,200 years. 99
>
> —Nanomedicine researcher Robert Freitas, Jr.

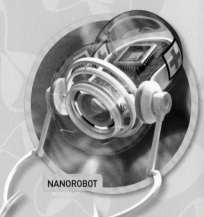

NANOROBOT

OUT OF STEP

Although it's happening much too slowly to see, the human species is continuing to evolve— and it would continue to do so during your immortal life. Eventually, you'd be the last member of the *Homo sapiens* species as humanity around you developed larger brains, saucer eyes, or spindly fingers. At least you'd stand out at a party!

Could it Happen?

In the next 20 to 30 years, doctors could begin injecting patients with microscopic medical robots—called "nanorobots"—that will swim through the bloodstream like a swarm of mechanical bees, replacing old cells and curing diseases. "By using annual checkups and cleanouts and some occasional major repairs by nanorobots," says author and nanomedicine researcher Robert Freitas, Jr., "your biological age could be restored once a year to a more or less constant physiological age that you choose. [This would] sever forever the link between calendar time and biological health."

Body

Oddities

What if you never stopped eating?

The good news is you won't keel over if you treat every meal like an all-you-can-eat buffet, although you'll probably wish you never reached for that 42nd slice of pizza. Your body has a protective mechanism that kicks in when your stomach reaches its capacity—about 1.5 quarts (1.4 L)—of solids and liquids. You'll start to get a queasy feeling known as nausea before your gag reflex engages and your stomach ejects all 16 helpings. Competitive eaters can short-circuit this reflex to reach the stomach's maximum capacity of about 1.3 gallons (5 L), at which point the stomach can actually rupture—with potentially fatal results. The lesson here: Pass up on pigging out.

What if you stopped blinking?

You don't need to think to blink—it's an automatic reflex that blocks dust and flushes away lubricating tears produced by ducts in the corners of our eyes. Adults blink about 15 times per minute, and our rate of blinking slows when we read (which is why our eyes tire after tackling a long book) or focus on a distant object. No matter how hard you try not to blink, the need to flush your eyes will eventually trump your willpower. Fighting the reflex isn't pleasant, either. Fergal "Eyesore" Fleming, a staring-competition champion who once kept his peepers peeled for an amazing 40 minutes and 59 seconds, likened the sensation to "getting a tattoo on my eyeball."

What if you stopped sleeping?

No one has ever actually died from lack of sleep. (One man perished after staying awake for 11 days, but doctors suspect other factors played a role in his death.) Avoid hitting the hay for a few days, however, and you'll soon suffer the consequences: crankiness, clumsiness—even hallucinations. Your brain will go on strike, and easy tasks will become supremely difficult until you turn in and switch off. It turns out your waking hours are crammed with activities and tasks that give your noggin a real workout. Researchers have found that all that processing causes chemicals to clutter your brain. A good night's sleep clears your head—literally. While you snooze, your brain goes into housekeeping mode, flushing the toxins and preparing itself for a busy day of deep thinking. About 5 percent of people—known as "short sleepers"—have a genetic condition that lets them get by with much less sleep than the average person.

Body Myths BUSTED!

What if you crossed your eyes for an hour? Despite the warnings from Mom, your eyes won't get stuck that way—although you'll probably get a headache.

What if you made a face for too long? You'll look pretty silly until you unscrunch your features, but then your face will resume its normal non-silly expression.

What if you accidentally swallowed your chewing gum? It won't really sit in your stomach for seven years. Like clockwork, your belly will empty its contents—including that glob of gum—into the intestine for further digestion and eventual disposal.

What if you never stopped growing?

You'd spend a lot of moolah on custom-fitted clothing, that's for sure. The average growth rate (not including growth spurts) for boys and girls is about 2.5 inches (6.4 cm) per year until they reach 17 or so and stop growing. Now, if you were to continue growing past your teens until you reached a ripe old age of 79 (the average life expectancy in the United States), you'd eventually add another 13 feet (4 m) to your current potential height, which would put you at about eye level with the chimney on a two-story house. Height is only half the story here, because you'd also put on weight as you grew. By the time you reached 79, you'd have put on an extra 341 pounds (155 kg)!

What if you had a prehensile tail?

You'd become the ultimate multitasker—if you didn't mind holes in your jeans.

Howler monkeys have them. So do opossums and ant-eaters, kinkajous and tree pangolins, chameleons and seahorses. All these cute critters possess an astounding appendage known as a prehensile tail: a specialized tail that has evolved to grasp objects. Monkeys use their long, skinny tails to dangle from branches, which frees their arms to grab tasty leaves. Baby opossums hang from their tails when they sleep. Seahorses wrap theirs around rocks and corals to anchor themselves in strong currents. Tree branches and sea currents might not factor into your daily life, but surely you could find a few uses for an extra appendage ...

Get a Grip

Give yourself a hand. No, really—give yourself an extra hand! A prehensile tail is like a bonus arm on your backside, able to serve all sorts of functions depending on its design. The animal kingdom's most multipurpose prehensile tail belongs to spider monkeys, howler monkeys, woolly monkeys, and other tree-dwelling New World monkeys of Central and South America. Strong, flexible, and tipped with a hairless "friction pad" that senses pressure and grips like a finger (it even has fingerprint-like ridges), this tail type functions like a fifth limb for these nimble monkeys.

And it's this style of Swiss army appendage that you would want. Naturally, it would boost your tree-climbing abilities, swinging you from branch to branch and even acting as a built-in safety harness when you just want to hang around. Your tail's fingerlike friction pad could swipe your smartphone's touch screen, freeing up your hands for other tasks. Of course, you could use your tail like a third arm to carry books or groceries, swat away flies, or simply open the door if your hands are full. Your tail's long length relative to your height means you could use it to snag objects off high shelves or prop it against the ground as a sort of portable chair. With such a super tail at your disposal, you'd never again need to stoop to scoop up something dropped or ask a friend to scratch a hard-to-reach itch.

HOWLER MONKEY

Side Effects Include ...

FOUL PLAY

Prehensile tails would throw the sports world for a loop. Basketball players, for instance, could block shots with their fifth limbs and use their tails for a leg up during slam dunks. Soccer leagues would need to decide if tails counted as hands or feet. Tennis players could grip an extra racket, turning singles games into doubles. Spectators, meanwhile, could hang from stadium rafters during crowded games.

TAIL TELLS

In the animal world, tails play an important role in communication. Leopards, for instance, flash the white undersides of their tails when they're finished stalking an animal, sort of like a flag of truce. Dogs use their tails to communicate their emotional states, from happiness to—is that a squirrel?! Imagine wagging your new tail when you're happy or combining tail gestures with your hand gestures for maximum emphasis (such as a super shrug).

HOLE TRUTH

Monkeys have it easy: They don't wear pants. You, on the other hand, would need clothes that accommodate your new appendage. Cutting a hole in the seat of your pants is only part of the solution. After all, you couldn't have that tail of yours exposing your backside when it wriggled around. (Ever hear of "plumber's crack"? Prehensile crack would be worse.) Clothing designers would have their hands full figuring out how to avoid wardrobe malfunctions with these tails.

Could it Happen?

Tales of humans with tails go back to ancient times, but the truth is we all have tails at the very earliest stages of our development. At around four weeks old, a human embryo develops a tiny tail that dissolves within eight weeks. Very rarely, and for reasons scientists don't understand, these tails don't melt away, and the baby is born eight months later with a nub of a tail up to five inches (13 cm) long. More common in boys than girls, these tails grow from the tailbone and actually have tiny muscles that let them twitch and curve slightly. They don't provide any of the gripping abilities of prehensile tails, however, and doctors typically remove them with a simple operation.

What if

Zits! Stained pits! Serious itch! Life would really start to stink!

Gross but true: The idea of a daily bath is relatively new. Ordinary people during the Middle Ages snubbed a regular scrub-a-dub-dub because they feared that cleaning their skin might invite evil into their bodies. Rich nobles traveled with their own bathtubs, but they rarely used them. England's Queen Elizabeth I boasted that she bathed once a month, "whether she needed it or not." But while soap and hot water were a luxury before the mid-19th century, people still took time to scour their bodies clean with special scraping tools, clumps of ash, or occasional dips in lakes or streams (citizens of the Roman Empire were unusual in that they scrubbed daily in elaborate public baths). But what if you cut out the cleaning routine completely?

Stench Warfare

Within a few days of your final shower, friends and family will begin detecting a foul fog in your general vicinity. You might think your sweat glands are responsible for your stink, but that's not really fair. More than 2.5 million glands in your skin ooze sweat to cool your body and flush out waste. All of that liquid is odorless when it's first secreted, but these secretions are a banquet for bacteria. Millions of microscopic life-forms munch on your sweat and produce stinky micro-poop—hence, B.O.—until you scrub them away in the shower—a shower that you're now skipping!

Aside from the pee-yew aroma they produce, these bacteria are harmless as long as they stick to the surface of your

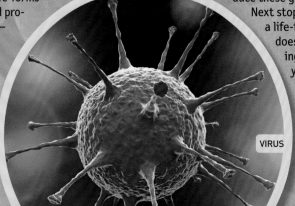

VIRUS

skin. But as you become filthier and filthier, you'll start to develop itchy rashes. Microscopic molds, yeasts, and other plantlike pathogens thrive in wet, warm places like our armpits, belly buttons, and the dank spaces between our toes. They feed on our sweat and dead tissues and produce wastes that irritate our skin. If you happen to scratch too hard and accidentally tear your skin, you can introduce these germs to your bloodstream. Next stop: the hospital! And if a life-threatening infection doesn't scare you into lathering up and hosing off, wait'll your hair morphs into a greasy mop plagued by itchy blizzards of dead skin known as dandruff. Yeah, but who needs a social life anyway?

Side Effects Include ...

DIRTY DUDS

In addition to your "eccrine" sweat glands that secrete salty sweat to cool your skin, your body has special "apocrine" glands in your hairiest parts that produce a yellowish liquid. Without your daily shower, the job of sopping up this nasty stuff will fall to your attire. Soon, every T-shirt you own will have matching pit stains.

ZIT FIT

As if your room-clearing odor isn't bad enough, your unscrubbed skin will soon begin erupting with every adolescent's enemy number one: pimples. Millions of hair follicles cover your body and produce protective oils, but it takes just one clog to create a zit. Without regular baths to keep those pores unclogged, bacteria and oil will combine into a repulsive pus that erupts when you give your new pimple a squeeze.

FILTHY AND FINE

While skipping baths for years can make you sick, missing the occasional scrubbing might actually be good for you. Those oils we mentioned above actually kill germs while moisturizing your skin. Scouring those oils away with a scrub brush can leave your skin dry, sterile of good bacteria (yes, some bacteria are good for you!), and vulnerable to the sun's damaging rays. The lesson here: Scrub away the stink, but don't overdo it!

Could it Happen?

Absolutely. In fact, the world record for the longest stretch between scrubbing is held by an Iranian man who hasn't bathed in 60 years (he believes that washing makes you ill, so he literally avoids bathtubs like they'll give him the plague). Despite six decades of sooty buildup on his skin, the man insists that he's happy with his simple life. Of course, just because you can set a world record for something doesn't mean you should—especially if you don't want to subject your social circle to the side effects of a life without soap and water.

Power Up

Superhero Origin Stories for Real ...

What if you were bombarded by cosmic rays?

In the comic books: Scientist Reed Richards, along with his pal Ben Grimm, girlfriend Susan Storm, and her brother Johnny, all blast off in an experimental spaceship—and right into a storm of cosmic radiation. They return to Earth with fantastic powers, from stretchy bodies to invisibility to rock-covered skin—and stick together as the Fantastic Four superhero team.

In real life: They might sound more like science fiction than science fact, but cosmic rays are a real phenomenon faced by space travelers. These superfast charged particles originate from far outside our solar system, cast off from the explosions of dying stars. Instead of granting cool superpowers like in the comics, however, cosmic rays can actually sap a person's abilities. Studies show that these rays cause brain damage and dull reaction times. Long-term exposure can even damage eyesight. Fortunately for us Earthlings, our planet's magnetic field protects us from this dangerous radiation. Astronauts in space may face the same storms that transformed the Fantastic Four—except without the fantastic results.

What if you were a mutant?

In the comic books: It's not lab accidents or toxic-waste spills that give comic-book "mutants" such as the X-Men abilities ranging from instant healing to mastery of storms. These heroes and villains are born this way, thanks to a quirk in their genetic structure.

In real life: They may not be able to summon storms or slice through steel with indestructible claws, but real-life mutants do exist. In fact, mutations are crucial to the process of evolution. Everything you see in the mirror—from your height to your hair color—is written into your DNA, spiraling chains of proteins called genes found in every cell in your body. Occasionally an organism is born with a mutation—or alteration—to its genetic structure. Helpful mutations are passed along to offspring, which leads to the evolution of new species better adapted for survival. About 12,000 years ago, for example, a mutation allowed humans to chug cow milk without getting sick. This ability was enormously beneficial to our survival, but it's not as exciting as, say, extra-thick bones that resist breaking, incredible endurance, naturally larger muscles, or a high tolerance for pain—all real mutations that people are born with today.

What if you were bitten by a radioactive spider?

In the comic books: The chomp of a radiation-blasted arachnid grants science-whiz Peter Parker superhuman strength and agility, as well as amazing wall-walking abilities, in the origin story of Spider-Man.

In real life: Even if radiation really did supercharge your body with stupendous abilities (it doesn't), a bite from a radioactive spider would deliver all pain and no gain in powers. A spider's bite—even the bite from a tarantula the size of a catcher's mitt—wouldn't transmit sufficient radiation to affect your body in any way, good or bad. And the fangs' effects would depend on the species: mild itchiness from most spiders, nausea and achy muscles from a black widow, or death within an hour from a Sydney funnel-web spider. Not even Spider-Man would want to tangle with one of those.

What if you were struck by lightning?

In the comic books: After getting zapped by lightning while working with chemicals in his lab, crime-scene investigator Barry Allen gains the ability to run, think, and react at superfast speeds. He dons a snappy red costume and becomes the Flash, a crime-fighting superhero who can even outrun Superman.

In real life: Lightning strikes about 2,000 people worldwide each year, and 9 out of every 10 victims survive with symptoms ranging from memory loss to dizziness to bizarre scars. Some survivors claim the bolt from the blue imbued them with powers ranging from superstrength to mind reading, although such claims have never been proved. Author Michele Young-Stone, who was struck by lightning when she was 11, says she can now feel when a storm is coming. "The hair on my arms stands up," she says. When thunder roars, head indoors.

What if you had **gills** like a **fish**?

Breathing underwater wouldn't be a problem. Living underwater, however …

Earlier in this chapter, you got the bad news that a pair of wings wouldn't help you reach new heights. (Bummer!) So would a set of gills help you achieve great depths? Breathe easy: The answer is yes. But while winged flight proved impossible, at least it's a task tuned for Earth's atmosphere—an environment for which humans have evolved. Life underwater requires many adaptations that we lack. Gills, it turns out, are just the beginning …

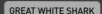

GREAT WHITE SHARK

Wet and Wild

Breathe in. Breathe out. Take pride in that swelling in your chest. Those are your lungs: a miraculous pair of balloon-like organs that absorb oxygen into your bloodstream with every breath you take. Most animals that live on land—and a few (such as reptiles and marine mammals) that live in the water—have lungs just like you. Aquatic animals such as fish and amphibians in their early stages of development, on the other hand, have gills: special organs located behind their mouths. As water passes over them, gills filter oxygen from the water directly into the fish's bloodstream.

For human aquanauts, gills offer an easier and safer alternative to breathing underwater than bulky air tanks. Scuba systems deliver air under extreme pressure, which can lead to a dangerous buildup of gases in the diver's tissues (scuba divers must limit their dive times or they risk painful illnesses and confusion). Gills sidestep these dangers because they don't deal with compressed gases; oxygen is filtered at the same pressure as the water around it. But gills do come with another complication—and this one's a doozy.

Have you ever heard of fish described as cold-blooded animals? That doesn't mean they're merciless minnow-chomping monsters. Fish require much less energy—and, therefore, less oxygen—than humans because they don't need to maintain their bodies at a constant temperature. Humans, on the other hand, are warm-blooded creatures. Maintaining our body temperatures requires more energy—and oxygen—than cold-blooded fish need, and more oxygen requires larger gills. How large? Try 16 feet (5 m) long, according to Andreas Fahlman, a biologist with Spain's L'Oceanogràfic aquarium. Like your wings in the scenario at the start of the chapter, your gills here would be the largest part of your body. But at least they would work!

Sea Changes:
Adaptations for Life in the Deep

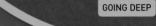
GOING DEEP

DEEP FREEZE
"Keeping warm will be a huge issue given our heat loss in the water," says marine biologist Robin Baird. Marine mammals keep toasty with an insulating layer of blubber, which you can simulate with a thick wet suit.

SEA SAW
Human eyes have adapted to see clearly in the air, not underwater. Masks and goggles provide a barrier of air between our eyes and the water, resulting in crystal-clear vision—as long as the water isn't murky. Then you'd wish you had the sonar-like "echolocation" abilities of dolphins and whales.

THIN FINS
Your giant gills, heavy wet suit, and sonar system might make life in the deep doable, but it wouldn't make it less dangerous. In the sea, with your lanky limbs and rubbery suit, you would look more like a sickly sea lion— a favorite snack of the great white shark. "Humans can't swim very fast," says Baird, "and just having webbed feet wouldn't make that much of a difference."

Could it Happen?

Every marine mammal on Earth—from manatees to porpoises to blue whales—evolved with lungs for a reason: Gills don't cut it when it comes to filtering enough oxygen from the water to keep a warm-blooded animal alive. And while it's true that human embryos develop gill-like slits in the womb, these slits have nothing to do with breathing and are more like folds of skin. If you're waiting for someone to invent artificial gills that filter oxygen out of the water, don't hold your breath (any contraptions you find online are just elaborate hoaxes). In fact, holding your breath—or breathing compressed air out of a scuba tank—is still your best option for wandering beneath the waves.

Chapter 2:
WONDERS OF THE WORLDS

Outer space is more than just a really big place—it's an endless source of what-if scenarios. Earthlings have barely dipped their toes in what astronomer Carl Sagan called the "cosmic ocean," and much of what lies above our planet's atmosphere falls into the category of the "great unknown." Suit up and dive into the cosmic ocean as we explore strange new worlds, seek out new life, and boldly go skydiving where no one has skydived before.

HOME SWEET HOME

What if you grew up in outer space?

What Would Happen if...

What if

Space is a great place to visit, but you wouldn't want to live there.

SAM, A RHESUS MONKEY, AFTER RETURNING FROM A RIDE ABOARD A SPACECRAFT

Before the first manned space flights of the 1960s, NASA crewed its craft with a small zoo's worth of animals, from fruit flies to mice, pooches to chimpanzees—and not because a squirrel monkey looks cute in a space suit. Scientists weren't sure if people could survive the trip! "They didn't even think that humans could consume and digest food properly without gravity," says astrobiologist Betul Kacar. Since then, hundreds of people have launched into space and made it their temporary home—some for longer than a year. But nobody has been born beyond the boundary of Earth's atmosphere (the youngest astronaut was 25 years old and fully grown). What would happen to a baby born on a space station or a ship traveling between worlds? Time to blast off and grow up!

Weight Watcher

Doctors examining astronauts upon their return from space made an important discovery: Gravity, just like your daily serving of veggies and a good night's sleep, is good for you. And while Earth's gravitational field is only slightly weaker in orbit, astronauts feel weightless in space because they're in a constant state of falling around the planet (the same goes for travelers between planets while they coast between course corrections). Without the weight of the world to work against, muscles begin to wither—as much as 5 percent each week. Bones become brittle. Without gravity's constant downward pull, blood pools in the head and gives the face a puffy appearance. In response, the body begins to produce less blood.

Now imagine if you grew up in this alien environment. Your muscles would grow only as strong as

needed to push off of walls and drift through the chambers of the ship. Your bones might grow at odd angles, weak and long. You would certainly stand taller than, say, your twin brother on Earth. Astronauts return home about two inches (5 cm) taller until gravity reasserts itself and scrunches their spines.

Friends on Earth could blast off for a visit, but you could never drop by to see them. Astronauts who return from long stints in orbit often leave the reentry vehicle in a wheelchair. Recovery can take months. As a kid who grew up in a weightless environment, you would slump beneath the full force of Earth's gravity. Bones would break. You would be too weak to walk. No longer an Earthling, you would be part of a new generation of explorers charged with charting the solar system for your ancestors back on Earth.

Side Effects Include ...

SUN BURNED

Space has its own weather: storms of charged particles cast off from the sun. Earth's ozone layer and magnetic field shield us from these storms, which can cause diseases such as cancer, but anyone growing up in space isn't so lucky. Such radiation can also introduce mutations—or changes—into humans traveling between worlds. Through time, these mutations might create a new species of humans better suited for life in space.

LACK OF SUPER VISION

Any space station is a site for sore eyes. Astronauts often report seeing flashes when their eyes are closed, which is actually cosmic rays from the space between stars. Long-term exposure to this radiation can form vision-impairing cataracts in the eyes. Weightlessness, meanwhile, actually changes the shape of the eyes and puts fluid pressure on the optic nerve. Children raised in space will likely be resigned to a life of thick glasses or contact lenses.

HEART STARTER

Not all of free fall's effects on the body are bad for your health. Without gravity to pump against, the heart doesn't have to work so hard to pump blood—and that's a good thing for people prone to heart disease. "Some have conjectured that weightlessness can prolong the lives of people with certain cardiovascular [or heart] problems," Kacar says.

Could it Happen???????

If humanity is ever going to colonize the solar system—and beyond—then children will inevitably be born in the weightless hulls of long-distance ships or on planets with low gravity. Fortunately for infant spacefarers, technology can counteract some of the problems of a weightless childhood. Astronauts in orbit have strapped themselves to treadmills, hefted special "weightless" weights, and sealed themselves in body-encasing vacuums to work their muscles and strengthen their bones. As gravity-simulating technology improves, space-raised Earthlings might even be able to take a walk on the planet of their grandparents. "They might require the use of [a muscle-boosting] artificial exoskeleton to visit the Earth," says Kacar.

ROBOTIC EXOSKELETON

What if

Even the smallest life-forms would be a big deal.

Sorry, UFO seekers. As far as the scientific evidence goes, we Earthlings live in a lonely universe. Our probes and rovers have uncovered no creepy-crawlies on Venus, no plants sprouting from the lunar soil, and nary a microbe on Mars. And decades of listening for radio transmissions from alien civilizations have turned up nothing but one unusual signal—named the "Wow! signal"—detected briefly in 1977. But that doesn't mean there's no place like home.

Astronomers and agrobiologists, scientists who study the possibility of alien life, are using high-tech tools to peer into the distant corners of our galaxy. Some think it's only a matter of time before we find evidence of life. When we do, it might be next door ...

Close to Home

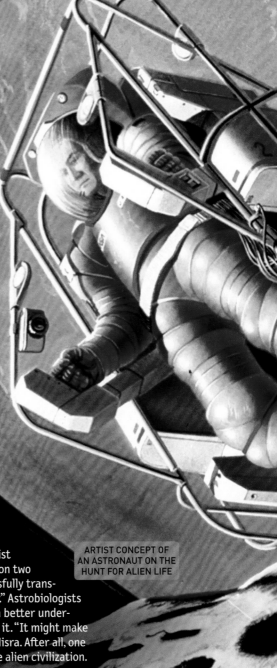

Biologists have discovered unusual organisms in harsh environ-ments, from Arctic ice to volcanic vents deep below the ocean's surface, right here on Earth, and these conditions exist on neighboring planets in our own solar system. Mars was once home to seas and rivers. The frozen surfaces of Jupiter's moon Europa and Saturn's moon Enceladus hide planet-spanning oceans. If our probes to these worlds find life-forms—alive or long dead and fossilized—they will most likely be itty-bitty.

But even the discovery of microscopic organisms would have huge implications. "It could indicate two things," says astrobiologist Jacob Haqq-Misra. "The first is that life developed independently on two separate planets in the solar system. The other is that life successfully trans-ferred from one planet to another by catching a ride on a meteor." Astrobiologists call this process "panspermia." Evidence of it would give humans a better under-standing of the origin of life—and even how we should search for it. "It might make us think more carefully about how we explore space," says Haqq-Misra. After all, one sneeze from a sick astronaut might wipe out the seeds of a future alien civilization.

ARTIST CONCEPT OF AN ASTRONAUT ON THE HUNT FOR ALIEN LIFE

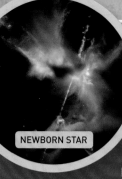
NEWBORN STAR

Far, Far Away

The universe might be teeming with life—even intelligent life—but the mind-boggling distances between billions of stars in billions of galaxies make it nearly impossible to detect signs of civilization on faraway worlds. It would take thousands of years to travel to the closest star outside our solar system using modern spaceship technology, so the best we can do is listen for space-based radio broadcasts and scan the heavens for Earthlike planets or space oddities such as "Dyson swarms." Named after theoretical physicist Freeman Dyson, these alien megastructures span entire solar systems and might be detected by the shadows they cast as they orbit their sun.

The discovery of any sign of intelligent life would mark the start of a new era for humanity—an era in which we know we're no longer alone in the universe. "It might even give us a new way of thinking about our common identity as 'Earthlings,'" says Haqq-Misra. "Now that we know there is another form of intelligence out there, which might help us think more seriously about our long-term future."

The next step: communication. But that's not easy considering that space is so vast and radio communications are limited by the speed of light (it would take eight years just to send a message and get a response from Earth's nearest star). And that's assuming we could figure out what our alien neighbors were saying. "We might be able to develop a common language, perhaps based on mathematics and basic physics," says Haqq-Misra, "but the light-year distances between us and them would make these conversations take years or even generations!"

66 **If we discover extinct life on Mars, that might give us hope to do a better job managing our own planet.** 99
—Astrobiologist Jacob Haqq-Misra

Could it Happen? ?

EYE IN THE SKY: THE KEPLER

Using the space-based Kepler telescope, astronomers are scouring the galaxy for Earthlike "exoplanets" capable of supporting life. They've discovered thousands of candidate worlds—some capable of supporting intelligent alien life. Meanwhile, NASA will continue probing our own solar system for life-forms living or long dead. The Search for Extraterrestrial Intelligence—or SETI project—continues to scan the universe for radio signals from alien civilizations. Of particular interest: our galaxy's 150 or so "globular clusters," or dense gatherings of stars at least 10 billion years old. Each cluster's extreme age and the relatively small distances between stars would give an alien civilization time and space to develop starships and colonize their stellar neighbors. All we can do is watch, listen, and wait.

What if

Let's make sure it has the right stuff before you blast off ...

Cup holders? Check! Home-theater system? Check! Any spaceship worthy of a joyride to Jupiter (and beyond) will need all the comforts of a high-tech home. After all, this vessel will serve as your living room, bedroom, bathroom, and kitchen—not to mention your source of air, water, light, and heat—for months or even years. But before you hop into the pilot's seat of your personal Millennium Falcon and lay in a course for the second star to the right, let's make sure this starship is shipshape and stocked with these state-of-the-art components ...

Propulsion System

Dashing spaceship captains in sci-fi flicks zoom from star system to star system faster than you can say "Punch it, Chewie!" In real life, our most advanced probes rely on solar-powered ion engines that convert electricity into thrust to gradually reach speeds of about 90,000 miles an hour (145,000 km/h). That might sound zippy, but it's only the tiniest fraction of the speed of light—the universal speed limit—and much too slow for travel beyond the planets in our solar system. At this speed, it would take months to reach our planetary neighbor Mars and tens of thousands of years to reach Proxima Centauri, the nearest star to our solar system. Fortunately, engineers are researching new propulsion systems—such as radiation-catching "solar sails" and even space-bending "warp drives"—that might one day get your ship up to light speed ... and beyond.

Shielding System

Asteroids aren't the biggest threat to your ship. You also need protection from the threats you can't see: supersonic pebble-size micrometeorites that do more than scratch your ship's paint job. They can actually puncture the hull, exposing your cozy habitat module to the icy, airless, lethal vacuum of space. Fortunately, your ship is equipped with a layer of bulletproof material set apart from the main hull to absorb the shock of micrometeorite strikes. Variations of this shield—named the Whipple shield after its inventor, Fred Whipple—have protected NASA's spacecraft for decades. Meanwhile, scientists are working on "self-healing" hulls lined with chemicals that plug punctures.

Habitat Module

Living space comes at a premium in outer space (the heavier your ship, the more fuel you'll need to carry to propel it through space), but your weightless environment means you can Velcro your sleeping back to the ceiling to create a bedroom and unfold a treadmill from the wall for an instant gym. A water-recycling system similar to the one on the International Space Station is essential to reclaim every drop of wastewater—including your toothbrushing spittle, the sweat in the air, and even your pee. Your pantry is stocked with the same freeze-dried squeeze bags of corned beef, PB&Js, and other instant treats packed aboard current space missions. Living in space burns more energy—your muscles are never truly at rest in a weightless environment—but you better resist the urge to pig out. No pizza delivery in interplanetary space!

NASA'S DEEP SPACE ATOMIC CLOCK

Navigation System

Traveling from A to B in a spaceship requires complex calculations—literally, rocket science—to "slingshot" from planet to planet (or moon) across the solar system using the gravity of each heavenly body. (The Voyager mission of the 1970s, for example, took advantage of a rare alignment of Jupiter, Saturn, Uranus, and Neptune to shave off nearly 20 years of travel time.) Taking a wrong turn in space could leave you marooned on a moon or plummeting into the crushing depths of a gas giant, so you'll want something fancier than a PlayStation 4 plotting your trajectories. The key piece of your navigation system: an accurate clock that syncs via radio with clocks back on Earth to provide pinpoint navigational data, sort of like the GPS system for the family car. Your ship will carry NASA's new "Deep Space Atomic Clock," an ultraprecise clock not much bigger than a hamburger.

Want fries with that freeze-dried burger? Print them out! NASA engineers are working on a machine that replicates hundreds of different meals using bags of raw ingredients that you load into the machine like a printer cartridge.

HOME AWAY FROM HOME

What if

You better start thinking of something good to say when you land!

Astronomers peering at Mars with primitive telescopes in the 17th and 18th centuries saw signs of life everywhere. Seas! Continents! Canals that carried water to Martian farms! Modern orbital probes and robot landers sent to investigate the red planet revealed the truth: a planet with no signs of life (so far!) but no shortage of mysteries. Robot rovers and orbital telescopes can only do so much. To solve the red planet's riddles, a team of scientists will need to go dig in the dust themselves with their own space-suited hands. What if you were the first Earthling to sift through Martian soil?

Ready for Launch

Training for any job in the space program—let alone a trip to Mars—can never start too early, especially when it comes to your studies of science and math. NASA requires its astronaut candidates to have a bachelor's degree in engineering, biological science, physical science, or mathematics. Mission commanders need an additional thousand hours behind the stick of a jet aircraft. Private spaceflight companies are looking for candidates who can adapt to new situations and solve problems while keeping a cool head. Make the cut and you'll undergo seven years of astronaut training and simulated Martian living before finally blasting off for the six-month trip to the red planet. Oh, and make sure to read the fine print before signing on: At least one planned mission—a Dutch project called Mars One—is a one-way ticket. You'll become a permanent Martian!

Famous First Words

Once your training is out of the way and you've made the team for the Mars mission, your biggest challenge might be coming up with what to say when you step out the airlock and into the history books as the first human to walk on another planet. You'll want something snappy but meaningful, clever but not too cute. Neil Armstrong, the first man to walk on the moon, became a hard act to follow when he said his famous line as he dropped off the lunar lander's ladder in 1969: "That's one small step for [a] man, one giant leap for mankind." Good luck topping that. And no pressure. You'll only have the eyes of the entire world on you.

NEIL ARMSTRONG, FIRST MAN ON THE MOON

Must-See Mars Attractions

Olympus Mons: The tallest volcano in the solar system, this Martian mountain is nearly three times taller than Mount Everest. Trekking up its gradual slope would be easy in gravity one-third of Earth's.

Hale Crater: Mars was once home to seas and riverbeds that astronomers later confused for canals. Recently, astronomers discovered evidence of salt water trickling down the walls of this crater. Might the water harbor alien microorganisms?

Valles Marineris: More than 2,500 miles (4,023 km) long and as much as 125 miles (200 km) across, the Valles Marineris is the grandest canyon in the solar system—large enough to stretch from the Pacific Coast to the Atlantic Coast of the United States.

OLYMPUS MONS

Seeing Red

After you finally touch down on the red planet, you'll notice it isn't even totally red! Browns, tans, golds, and flecks of green pop out as you scan the rocky, dusty, dune-laden landscape. Mars only looks red from far away because of rusting iron minerals in the rocks and soil. The soil blows into the air (occasionally in planetwide dust storms) to give the atmosphere a bloody tint. The atmosphere here was thicker in ancient times. Now, the air (mostly carbon dioxide) is too wispy to support water or hold much heat— and it's certainly too thin to breathe. If you were foolish enough to take off your space suit and stand on the equator at high noon, your toes would feel toasty but your face would be freezing. Welcome to life on another world!

Could it Happen?

Absolutely! With NASA planning to launch manned missions to Mars by the 2030s—and private space-flight projects scheming to send humans to Mars even sooner— chances are good chance that the first person to step foot on the red planet is already walking around on Earth. Maybe it's someone in your science class. Maybe it's the college kid working at the local burger joint. Maybe it's you?

Cosmic Errors

What if you stepped into space without your space suit?

Despite what you've seen in some scary sci-fi movies, your lungs wouldn't explode and your eyes wouldn't bulge from your skull. But direct exposure to space would be a lethal—and, as you'd expect, uncomfortable—experience if you didn't scramble back into your ship's airlock or plug any leaks in the ship's hull. Astronauts work in a hostile environment, after all. Outer space lacks air—and, therefore, air pressure, which is actually crucial to the function of lungs that have evolved to work in Earth's atmosphere. Space is also either lethally cold or deadly hot depending on whether an astronaut is in the sun or shade.

You wouldn't immediately suffocate, freeze, or fry if you stepped outside, but you would suddenly find yourself out of breath. The absence of air in space creates a vacuum that would suck all the breath from your lungs through your nose and mouth. All the tiny bubbles of oxygen in your blood vessels would begin to expand, causing your body to balloon in weird places (your face would begin to swell, for instance). The moisture on the surface of your eyes would bubble and sort of boil away. Unless you got back inside, you would quickly pass out and perish in less than a minute from a lack of oxygen. The lessons of this story: Never forget your space helmet!

Four Space Firsts

First person to orbit the Earth:
Soviet cosmonaut Yuri Gagarin, April 12, 1961

First selfie in space:
American astronaut Buzz Aldrin, November 1966

First person on the moon:
American astronaut Neil Armstrong, July 20, 1969

First American woman in space:
Sally Ride, June 18, 1983

What if you accidentally slipped while working outside the International Space Station?

This predicament is nearly impossible for one reason: All astronauts who step out the airlock connect themselves to the station with a steel tether. But if the tether snaps, don't panic! Kicking and flailing will only waste your air (you can't "swim" through space because there's nothing to push against with your limbs). Your space suit is like a tiny spaceship, re-creating all the comforts of home: air, air pressure, temperature control, cool water through a sippy straw, and even a potty.

Back when NASA's space shuttle still flew into orbit, the shuttle pilots could simply scoot over to pick you up. Today, all astronauts who step outside the International Space Station wear a sort of life jacket for spacewalking: the SAFER jet pack. Short for "Simplified Aid for EVA (Extravehicular Activity) Rescue," the SAFER has small thrusters that fire bursts of nitrogen to steer you back to safety. If your SAFER fails or runs out of gas, your friends back on the station have a backup plan: They'll combine multiple tethers and fly out to rescue you, then reel you back to the safety of the station. In the extremely unlikely event that they couldn't get to you, the station might eventually veer in your direction, depending on its own orbital trajectory—at which point you should earn a gold medal for history's greatest long jump.

ASTRONAUT CARL J. MEADE TESTS THE NEW SIMPLIFIED AID FOR EVA RESCUE (SAFER) SYSTEM SOME 130 NAUTICAL MILES ABOVE EARTH.

Star Tech: Spin-Off Space Inventions

Ear thermometers: NASA developed heat sensors that take your temperature without sticking a thermometer under your tongue.

Memory foam: The spongy material in your mattress was originally designed for aircraft seat cushions.

Artificial limbs: Research into robotic astronauts has led to more functional arms and legs for people who don't have them.

Invisible braces: Straightening your choppers no longer requires a mouthful of metal thanks to a tough, transparent plastic originally created for missile systems.

What if

Pack some freeze-dried snacks. It's a long way up!

T-minus 5, 4, 3, 2, 1 ... *bing*. Next stop: Low Earth orbit! The idea of riding an elevator up and away into space might sound like stupendous science fiction (and it was first made popular in a 1979 novel by sci-fi author Arthur C. Clarke), but the concept is neither new nor all that outlandish. Such an elevator was first proposed by a Russian scientist named Konstantin Tsiolkovsky in 1895, and it has since undergone many engineering studies proving it could work.

The idea is simple. Elevator builders would launch a construction satellite into geosynchronous orbit—the altitude at which an object's orbital speed matches the rotation of the Earth so that the object hovers above a fixed spot on the ground. The satellite would then lower a "seed ribbon" about 22,000 miles (35,400 km) long to Earth's surface, where workers would anchor it to a ground station. The satellite would simultaneously unspool a second seed ribbon straight up to about 60,000 miles (around 100,000 km) in space. Here, a counterweight made of obsolete satellites and other space junk would attach to the ribbon and hold it taut as it hurled around the Earth.

Robotic construction machines would scurry up and down this ribbon, reinforcing it with superstrong materials until it became a thicker tether tough enough to support the weight of "climber" cars built to ferry cargo and, eventually, passengers from the Earth all the way to space. Suddenly, a trip to orbit would become less costly and more environmentally friendly than a rocket that requires tremendous amounts of fuel just to lift satellites or a few people into orbit. Ready for a ride? Hop aboard for the long trip to the top ...

COMPUTER ARTWORK OF A CONSTRUCTION SATELLITE AT WORK

Ground Floor

The term "space elevator" isn't really that accurate. It's more like a high-speed railroad that rides into the sky. A climber car's interior reminds you of a train passenger car built for long trips, complete with comfy seats that unfold into beds, personal-entertainment screens, showers, and kitchens. Powered by a combination of solar energy and lasers fired from the ground station, each climber travels around 200 miles an hour (322 km/h) up the tether, which means a trip to geosynchronous orbit would take nearly five days. A journey all the way to the counterweight would last nearly two weeks. Hope you brought your toothbrush.

First Stop: Low-Earth Orbit

The ride up the tether is nothing like a train or plane trip on Earth—and not just because of the spectacular views. The sensation of gravity decreases gradually as you ascend, slowly at first and then more rapidly as you, the car around you, and the tether it's riding "fall" around the Earth in sync with the planet's rotation. Less than three hours after "takeoff," you'll reach a small space station at low Earth orbit at an altitude of around 500 miles (805 km). This place is little more than an observatory and tourist destination, perfect for lunch in low gravity or selfies in front of vistas of Earth. But your journey up the tether has only just begun. Turn the page to complete your trip ...

See next page for more!

Next Stop: Geosynchronous Orbit

Welcome to free fall, or the sensation of zero gravity. Keep a spacesickness bag in your pocket as you explore a space station that sprawls in every direction. You'll find workshops for servicing satellites, observatories for studying the heavens, a spaceport for receiving flights from across the solar system, and possibly a hotel and arenas for zero-gravity sports. You'd love to take in a game of free-fall football, but the climber is about to leave the station. You hop—or, rather, float—aboard and strap in for the last leg of your journey.

Final Stop: The Apex Anchor

A tingle builds in your stomach as you leave the geosynchronous station far behind and head for the counterweight at the end of the tether, 60,000 miles (100,000 km) in space. Suddenly, up begins to feel like down. As you approach the end of the line, centrifugal force takes hold and pulls you toward the ceiling of the climber, which is now on the floor. After several days of travel, you finally reach the counterweight—or "Apex Anchor." Here, in the artificial gravity created by the centrifugal force, you find a small station with a communications array that keeps tabs on mankind's colonies across the solar system. The station is not much to look at, but the view is spectacular. Look straight up through the skylights (remember that up and down are reversed here) and you can see Earth at the end of an impossibly thin ribbon. Now you just need to decide whether you want to board the climber for the long ride home, or hop aboard one of the station's small docked spaceships and explore the solar system.

Side Effects Include ...

GETTING THERE IS HALF THE FUN

Just reaching the ground station at the start of your trip will be an adventure. Elevator builders will anchor their ground stations in remote places—usually on the high seas away from hurricane-prone areas—along the Equator. Aircraft will be forbidden from entering elevator airspace for security reasons. That means you'll need to fly to some remote island, then take a boat to the station platform far out to sea.

LAUNCH PAD

If a spaceship docked outside the climber car detaches at just the right moment above the geosynchronous station, centrifugal force will fling the ship to the moon, Mars, the asteroid belt, and beyond. "This should open up tremendous possibilities to really explore and colonize much of the solar system," says Ted Semon of the International Space Elevator Consortium, which is organizing the construction of a space elevator.

AWAY FROM IT ALL: ARTIST RENDERING OF AN ELEVATOR GROUND STATION

MULTIWALLED CARBON NANOTUBE

Could it Happen???

At least two companies are planning to build space elevators by the year 2050. The only holdup is a lack of the superstrong material needed to build the tether. Scientists have devised several potential materials with exotic names like "carbon nanotubes" and "diamond nanothreads," but they haven't learned how to mass-produce these superstrong threads. "Once the chemists, physicists, and engineers figure out how to make these same materials into very long lengths, then the real planning can begin," Semon says. "It's only a matter of time, and I think 50 to 100 years is more than enough. We're all waiting as fast as we can."

What if

You won't hit the ground. The "ground" will hit you.

Daredevils who leap from airplanes don't get much time to enjoy the trip down. Unless they strap on oxygen masks and the other special gear needed to parachute from high altitudes without passing out, skydivers only free-fall for about a minute before it's time to pop the parachute and float safely to the landing zone. It's a small price to pay for living on a "terrestrial planet": one made of rocks, minerals, metals, and other tough stuff. Our solar system has four such planets: Earth, Mercury, Venus, and Mars—also known as the "inner planets" because they formed from debris that orbited closer to the sun about 4.6 billion years ago. But what if you took the plunge over a "gas giant": one of the four "outer planets" made of nothing but atmosphere? Would you just fall through a fluffy core of clouds and pop out the other side? Better look before you leap ...

Jumping **Jupiter**

For this scenario, we've set a course for the nearest gas giant: Jupiter. This ball of mostly hydrogen and helium is the biggest planet in our solar system—big enough to hold more than 1,300 Earths. It takes your ship about 13 months to travel from Earth to Jupiter, so you're probably itching to leap out the airlock and stretch your legs. The good news is you'll get about 25 minutes of free fall. The bad news is you won't have a happy landing.

You don't feel it here on Earth, but the air around you actually weighs something. Gravity is constantly pulling the Earth's atmosphere downward and toward the planet's core, and the weight of all that air above you creates pressure that builds as you get closer to the ground. Air is thickest and heaviest at sea level, where humans have evolved to live. The air pressure on Earth's surface is comfortable for us. On Jupiter, with its bottomless atmosphere and gravity nearly two-and-a-half times as strong as Earth's, the air pressure quickly builds to an uncomfortable squeeze.

As you sink deeper and deeper into Jupiter's clouds of ammonia and hydrogen atmosphere, the pressure—and temperature—keeps increasing around you. About 25 minutes into your free fall, as you plummet into darkness through clouds blocking out the distant sun, the air becomes so thick that it slows your fall. Soon the air pressure compresses the atmosphere into a molten liquid. Instead of slamming into the ground like on Earth, the air on Jupiter sort of thickens around you like boiling soup, squeezing and squeezing and squeezing, until you melt and become part of the liquid around you.

6

Side Effects Include ...

DANGER ZONE

Crushing air pressure is hardly the only hazard you'll face. Because of the planet's strong gravity, you'll fall too quickly and burn up in the planet's outer atmosphere unless you deploy a tiny parachute to slow your descent. What you'll really need is some sort of force field to deflect radiation more than a thousand times the lethal dose and temperatures that rival the surface of the sun as you sink into molten depths.

ALTERNATE ROUTES

Don't expect happier landings on the solar system's three other outer planets. Leap beneath the famous rings of gas giant Saturn and you'll fall into electrical storms the size of the United States. Neptune is home to the windiest weather in the solar system. Clouds of frozen methane whoosh as fast as a fighter jet through storms that would engulf all of Earth.

TICKET UPGRADE

You've probably figured out that a long leap out a spaceship airlock isn't the safest way to explore the outer planets. Consider an alternate form of travel: Science-fiction writers have proposed exploring the gas giants in hot-air balloons high above the crushing depths below. After all, clouds of lung-melting ammonia are much prettier when you peer at them through a porthole in air-conditioned comfort.

SATURN'S SKYDIVING WEATHER

GALILEO SPACECRAFT

Could it Happen?

Human astronauts haven't parachuted over Jupiter (and likely never will—on purpose), but our probes have. In 1995, the sensor-studded satellite Galileo plunged for 100 miles (161 km) into Jupiter's atmosphere before it was crushed 78 minutes into its fall. That same atmosphere ripped apart a comet in 1994, creating dark marks half the size of Earth in the planet's atmosphere.

What if

Some seriously strange stuff, and none of it good ...

Black holes are among the most fascinating objects in the universe, but don't bother scanning the skies for one. These matter-munching space oddities are invisible by their very nature. Astronomers only know black holes exist because they can observe their effects on nearby stars, planets, gas, and other space debris. The most common type of black holes (called stellar mass black holes) form when large stars—those about 20 times bigger than our own sun—run out of fuel and go "supernova," or explode. The dying star's core collapses under its own gravity until it scrunches into a tightly packed point known as a singularity. Despite its tiny size, the singularity packs a gravitational field nearly as strong as the giant star that created it. Like a cosmic whirlpool, the singularity sucks in anything—asteroids, planets, other stars, and even light (which is why they're invisible)—that gets too close. Uh-oh! You just got too close!

Falling Apart

Everything goes dark as your spaceship approaches the black hole's swirling "event horizon," or point of no return, about 4,000 miles (6,437 km) from the singularity. The gravitational tug here is so powerful that just the difference in gravity between the front of your ship and the back of it leads to a frightening effect with a funny name: "spaghettification." Your ship and everything in it become longer and thinner, stretching and stretching until something gives. Everything snaps into smaller and smaller bits that stretch into an impossibly thin and long line like a

Unless your vessel is equipped with a protective force field and artificial-gravity device—technologies that don't exist yet—to negate the deadly effects of spaghettification, you won't survive your maiden voyage into a black hole. Even if you did pass the event horizon, you'll never escape the singular-

PRESS PAUSE

As your ship approaches the singularity, it zips faster and faster until you approach the speed of light. Time slows and eventually stops. If you survived spaghettification, you could peek forward to see the star frozen in its perpetual collapse along with everything that has ever fallen into this particular black hole. Look behind and you'll see every-thing that will ever fall in after you. Told you things would get strange!

GOING NOWHERE FAST

Astrophysicists (and sci-fi writers) theo-rize that black holes can lead to alternate dimensions or serve as doors to shortcuts through the universe called wormholes. If you somehow survive your journey into the singularity, you might suddenly find yourself halfway across the galaxy—or in another galaxy altogether. Or black holes could just lead nowhere, the equivalent to jumping into a planet-smashing trash com-pactor. Astronomers just don't know.

THINK BIGGER

You think stellar black holes are awesome? Wait till you meet their big brothers. Astrono-mers suspect that "supermassive" black holes churn at the core of every galaxy in the uni-verse, including our own. Plunging into one of these monsters—which are millions (if not bil-lions) of times as massive as our sun—would give you more time to enjoy the ride before spaghettification stretched you to pieces.

BLACK HOLES PLAY TRICKS WITH SPACE AND TIME

Could it HaPPen?

Not anytime soon. Using today's space-ship technology, it would take hundreds of millions of years to reach the near-est known black hole, which is about 20,000 light-years away. (One light-year is how far light travels in a year.) These staggering stellar distances are a good thing. Black holes routinely shred plan-ets and inhale stars, and astronomers estimate that our galaxy is home to as many as 10 million to a billion of these destructive objects. We wouldn't want one dropping by our solar system.

What if

The farthest we Earthlings have ever journeyed from home is about 250,000 miles (402,000 km) during the manned moon missions of the 20th century. That's like leaving your house but never stepping off the welcome mat. To reach the edge of our universe, you'll need to go considerably farther than that in a ship that can defy physics to zip through space at speeds much faster than light. Here are the keys. Hop in!

2 light-years from home: Bidding the sun goodbye

With this last artifact of Earth's ingenuity behind you, you rocket through the Kuiper belt of icy bodies and the more distant region known as the Oort cloud, both sources of the comets that occasionally brighten the skies of Earth with their sun-blown tails of vapor. Once you blast past the last of these slushballs, you'll finally have escaped the gravity of the sun, now two light-years behind you. You transmit your achievement and a selfie back to Earth but don't stick around for a response (which would take four years to reach you).

11 billion miles from home: Entering interstellar space

Starting your trek in Earth orbit, you opt for the scenic route through the asteroid belt between Mars and Jupiter, then cross the orbits of the remaining outer planets (Saturn, Uranus, and Neptune). Four times farther out from the sun—about 11 billion miles (18 billion km)—you cross the "heliopause," the point where solar energies cast off by the sun can no longer be detected. The heliopause is considered the beginning of interstellar space, or the void between stars. The sun, now far behind you, is a speck compared to its former glory, although it's still by far the brightest object in the sky. Suddenly, a glint catches your eye ahead. You pull alongside the Voyager 1 probe: the farthest-traveling human-made object in the solar system—until now.

SO LONG, SOLAR STORMS!

VOYAGING INTO THE FINAL FRONTIER

2.5 million light-years from home: Exploring the galaxies

Traveling through deep interstellar space is a bit of a bore, really, so let's cut to the chase. After blasting outward from the dense core of older stars, dodging the crushing pull of black holes and the sensor-scrambling radiation of neutron stars, you eventually leave the galaxy and cruise through the "Local Group" of galaxies dominated by Andromeda, a spiral galaxy like our own Milky Way except home to as many as a trillion stars. Back on Earth, Andromeda is the farthest thing you can see with the naked eye on a clear night. Way out here, as you peek back toward home, the light hitting your eyeballs from your own galaxy left its stars millions of years before human beings even appeared on the fossil record.

CLUSTER OF STARS

BLACK HOLE ERUPTIONS

47 billion light-years from home: The end?

Eventually you reach the edge of the "observable universe," about 47 billion light-years from home and moving farther away all the time. Welcome to the edge of the universe—literally, the final frontier—as we see it from Earth using our most powerful telescopes. Here you find the most ancient galaxies, flung outward by the "big bang" that begat time and space 13.8 billion years ago. Because no one on Earth can see beyond this point, astronomers can only theorize what lies beyond. Perhaps a series of alternate universes? An endless expanse filled with an infinite number of galaxies? Nothing at all— not even time and space? Only one way to find out. Gunning the engines of your starship, you cross into the unknown.

4 light-years from home: Flying by our closest star

Reaching the boundary of our solar system is only the start of a much larger journey. The nearest star—Proxima Centauri—is at least two light-years away, part of the "Local Interstellar Cloud." This cluster of dust, gas, and stars (including our sun) lies in the Orion arm, a smaller spur between two of the major arms orbiting the core of our Milky Way galaxy, home to between 200 billion and 400 billion stars.

Chapter 3:
Second Nature

Curiosity might have killed the cat, but in this chapter, curiosity will help you see through that cat's eyes—plus have a powwow with a pod of dolphins, play fetch with a "de-extinct" woolly mammoth, and take your turn as babysitter in a wolf family. Unleash your curiosity and let your imagination run wild in this chapter that looks at the alternate worlds of wildlife.

What Would Happen if...

What if

The world would be a different place—and you wouldn't be around to see it.

Tyrannosaurus rex never saw it coming. Around 66 million years ago, an asteroid or comet nearly the size of San Francisco slammed into the seabed off the Yucatán Peninsula in Mexico at 45,000 miles an hour (72,420 km/h). Shock waves and tsunamis as tall as skyscrapers scoured nearby landmasses of all trees and dirt down to the bedrock, while the impact hurtled dust and vapor to the edge of Earth's atmosphere. Then things got really bad. A global heat wave was followed by a planetwide chill. Over the next few thousand years, roughly 75 percent of all species went extinct, including most of the dinosaurs. But what if that direct hit had been a miss?

END OF THEIR WORLD

You Who?

The dino-doomsday left a void for smarter, smaller animals to fill. Among them were the mammals. These furry creatures had scurried beneath the feet of dinosaurs for nearly 150 million years, scavenging for scraps while running for their lives. Suddenly the world was all theirs. Mammals took advantage of the situation by growing in size and diversifying into many of the species we know today: cats, dogs, horses, bats, and primates—the order of animals that eventually gave rise to gorillas, chimpanzees,

But if that asteroid had sailed past Earth, "there's no reason to think dinosaurs would have died out," says Stephen Brusatte, a paleontologist at the University of Edinburgh in Scotland. "They had been around for 160 million years and were doing fine. And without dinosaurs dying out, mammals would have never gotten their chance, and our ancestors wouldn't have evolved." In other words, you, your pooch, and everyone you know today owe their existence to a cosmic accident.

Side Effects Include ...

BYE-BYE, BIRDIES

ARCHAEOPTERYX

Chickens, parakeets, turkeys, ostriches—every bird you see today is actually a modern dinosaur. They evolved from a group of two-legged meat-eating dinosaurs that took to the skies on feathery wings about 150 million years ago. When the asteroid wiped out all the non-avian (or non-bird) dinosaurs 66 million years ago, early birds found themselves in a similar situation as mammals. Much smaller than their non-avian relatives, they were able to scavenge for food in a changing world. "But if birds never had that opportunity to evolve so quickly in the aftermath of a global catastrophe," says Brusatte, "maybe they wouldn't have developed the huge diversity such as the 10,400 species alive today."

DINO MIGHT

Before a space rock spoiled their party, dinosaurs were constantly evolving into new species and subgroups—such as meat-munching theropods, plant-eating sauropods, and beaked ornithischians—with distinct body shapes and behaviors. They had spread to every continent on Earth, and these subgroups would have continued to evolve as Earth's climate changed over the past 66 million years. "Who knows what these subgroups would have become," says Dr. Brusatte. "Some may have gotten bigger; others much smaller. Our imaginations can run wild."

VELOCIRAPTOR

DINO BRIGHT

Can you picture a dinosaur ordering out instead of pouncing on dinner? In the 1980s, paleontologist Dale Russell envisioned just such a brainy beast—a humanoid dinosaur with a big brain and three-fingered hands capable of wielding tools. He proposed that this "dinosauroid" could have evolved from a real species of ostrich-like dinosaurs called troodons that had relatively large brains and fingers that could grasp objects. If the troodons hadn't been wiped out by the asteroid, Russell figured, they might have continued to evolve into his theoretical dinosauroid over the next 66 million years. Other paleontologists are skeptical that dinosaurs would have evolved into such a humanoid form, but few doubt they could have developed greater intelligence.

Could it Happen?

DIRECT HIT

The question here isn't so much "Could it happen?" but "Could it happen again?" It's not a matter of if but when. Asteroids have smashed into every planet in the solar system. Scientists estimate that more than a million of these roving rocks orbit the sun in the asteroid belt between Mars and Jupiter. But when Jupiter's gravity tugs one of the larger asteroids loose and sends it tumbling toward the sun, we better watch out! Astronomers are scanning the skies to track any "near-Earth objects," including asteroids and comets that might drift too close to home. NASA has identified 90 percent of all the objects large enough to cause catastrophic damage if they struck our planet, including an asteroid named Apophis (after an ancient Egyptian demon of destruction) that will fly by in 2036. Later in this book, you'll find out how we might deflect a deadly hit from one of these space mountains.

What if

Millions of lives would be saved, but at what cost to the environment?

The next time you smack a mosquito that's nibbling on your neck, consider this: You were just bitten by the world's deadliest animal! These annoying winged insects have been slurping the blood of animals since the age of dinosaurs. Buzzing from person to person and jabbing them with their needlelike "proboscises," mosquitoes spread deadly diseases such as dengue fever and malaria, which kill nearly a million people each year. What if you could wipe out mosquitoes—or at least the 200 or so species that drink blood— with just a snap of your fingers?

Off the Menu

Imagine if you popped the hood of your parents' car and started pulling out parts. It wouldn't take long for the engine to sputter or burn too much gas or belch smoke. That's because all those parts work together in a system. Eliminating all mosquitoes might throw habitat systems out of whack in a similar way. After all, just because they're deadly doesn't mean mosquitoes are useless. They actually form an important part of the food chain.

All sorts of life-forms—bats, birds, fish, frogs, lizards, and even some plants—munch on these bloodsucking insects as an easy meal. Removing mosquitoes would knock some ecosystems out of balance. Fish that feed on mosquito larvae would starve, and animals that eat those fish would soon begin

to get hungry, too. An absence of mosquitoes would send shock waves up the food chain, all the way to us humans at the top.

But other tasty insects would multiply to fill the void left by mosquitoes—which aren't even the main course for many animals. Bats, for example, prefer to gobble up meatier moths. To them, mosquitoes are just a snack. Ultimately, scientists don't know all the consequences of a mosquito-free world. They're not even sure if a deadlier insect wouldn't take the mosquito's place. Researchers in Florida found that wiping out one species of mosquito in a region only opened the door for a species known for transmitting more dangerous diseases. The lesson of this scenario: It's best not to mess with Mother Nature.

Caribou Comfort

It's not just humans that suffer from mosquito infestations. In the Arctic, mosquitoes form such thick swarms that caribou actually choke on them. Eliminating these bloodsucking insects from the region might make life more comfortable for the caribou, but it would also disrupt their migratory paths, which in turn would affect the landscape in ways biologists can't predict.

Extra Life

Some scientists think the danger posed by mosquitoes outweighs any potential environmental damage that might arise from wiping them out. In a world without mosquitoes—and the diseases they spread—millions of people would be happier and healthier. Hospitals and clinics would be less crowded. The productivity of entire nations would increase. Fewer mosquitoes would result in more people.

CARIBOU

Could it Happen?

Wielding toxic fogs, sticky traps, and deadly chemicals, scientists have achieved major victories in the war against mosquitoes. In the early 1900s, for instance, they managed to suppress a species of disease-spreading mosquito in South America long enough for workers to finish the Panama Canal. Use of the pesticide DDT killed out all malaria-causing mosquitoes in the United States by 1949. But these pesticides came with nasty side effects: such as cancer in humans and damage to bird populations. They've since been banned in many countries. Now scientists are researching technologies that kill mosquitoes without causing harm to other species, but the very best they can hope for is population control rather than annihilation. Mosquitoes spawn in bodies of water big and small. To wipe them out, we would need to sop up every last puddle in the road. The best we can hope for is a world with fewer bloodsucking insects—and the diseases they spread.

ANTI-MOSQUITO FOGGING

Lost and Found

Buzz Killers!

Although honeybees need protection, scientists wouldn't mind saying bye-bye to another type of bee: African honeybees, better known as killer bees. This highly aggressive breed of honeybee—the product of an experiment to create a bee that makes more honey—escaped from a Brazilian laboratory in 1957 and has been heading north ever since. Killer bees pursue any threat until it drops—and then continue stinging and stinging and stinging! A swarm chasing a Texas man stung him more than a thousand times!

What if honeybees went extinct?

Starting in 2006, beekeepers across the United States noticed an alarming fact about their hives. Honeybees were fleeing their queens and colonies, never to return. The phenomenon—called "colony collapse disorder"—continued to spread, and by 2013 beekeepers were reporting average losses of 45 percent of their hives. Bee researchers are scrambling to figure out what's causing the disappearing act. Current suspects include parasites, viruses, pesticides, or a combination of all three.

Why should you care if some stinging insects say "Sayonara"? Unlike those pesky mosquitoes, honeybees are vital pollinators for everything from apples to almonds, avocados to onions (not to mention the source of all honey). Half of the fruits and veggies you find in the produce section of your local grocery store would suddenly be gone. Honeybees also pollinate the plants that feed livestock animals such as cows, pigs, and chickens. The flight of the honeybees could spell starvation for humans on a global scale!

What if we could bring extinct animals back to life?

The woolly mammoth, the dodo bird, the Caribbean monk seal—these animals are gone but not forgotten, hunted to extinction by humans. But science may have figured out a way of undoing our mistakes. Take the woolly mammoth, for instance. Scientists in America, South Korea, and Siberia (where mammoths once roamed in the thousands) are working on ways to "de-extinct" one of these furry, long-tusked elephant relatives, which have been gone for more than 10,000 years. First, the scientists need to extract cells from frozen mammoth carcasses discovered in the tundra. They'll implant these cells in an elephant, which will act as a surrogate mother for a baby mammoth-elephant hybrid. If all goes well, we could see the return of the woolly mammoth in a matter of years! What about bringing back more ancient animals, such as the dinosaurs? Don't believe everything you saw in the *Jurassic Park* movies. Unlike with more recently extinct species, scientists just don't have enough genetic material to resurrect *Tyrannosaurus rex*.

GRAY WHALE

WOOLLY MAMMOTH

AMUR TIGER

SOUTHERN WHITE RHINO

Making a Comeback: Species Saved From Extinction

Southern White Rhino
Population low point: Fewer than 100 animals lived in Africa in 1895.

Population today: Protected from ivory hunting, rhino numbers recovered to more than 20,000.

Amur Tiger
Population low point: Forty in the 1940s due to hunting for the tiger's fur and use in folk medicines.

Population today: Up to possibly 7,000 in their Russian range thanks to protection from poachers.

Gray Whale
Population low point: Whaling wiped out one of the three populations of this massive whale.

Population today: Although fewer than 150 gray whales live in the North Pacific, the population in the Eastern North Pacific has completely recovered.

What if

we could **speak** with **dolphins**?

Small talk will be easy. Deep conversations will be the tricky part ...

The mother dolphin began talking with her baby ... over a video chat! This special phone call—actually an experiment in dolphin communication—took place at an aquarium in Hawaii, U.S.A., where the mother and her two-year-old calf swam in separate tanks connected by a special underwater audio-video link. The two dolphins began squawking and chirping to each other: distinctive dolphin speak. "It seemed clear that they knew who they were talking with," says Don White, whose Project Delphis ran the experiment. "Information was passing back and forth pretty quickly." But what were they saying? That's what scientists have been trying to figure out for decades, studying wild and captive dolphins all over the world to decipher their mysterious language. What if they cracked the code?

BOTTLENOSE DOLPHIN

Conversation **Starters**

More than 30 species of dolphins—including orcas (aka killer whales) and the Atlantic bottlenose dolphin made famous on TV and in aquarium shows—roam the world's oceans and rivers. In many ways, they're just like you. As fellow mammals, they must swim to the surface to breathe air. They form close friendships and work together in groups called pods to accomplish tasks. And they talk to each other using what seems like a learned language of squawks, whistles, squeaks, and clicks. If we could suddenly understand what they were saying—and chat back—we could begin a conversation with the world's second smartest animal (after humans). We might unravel the mysteries of their complex social lives, explore their sense of history and culture, and ask them to share the hidden wonders of their

undersea world. But not before breaking the ice first. "I would like to know how they spend their day and what is important to them," says Denise Herzing, who has studied dolphin communication for 30 years in the Bahamas.

But just because we could communicate with dolphins doesn't mean we would understand everything they had to say. Dolphins and humans haven't shared a common ancestor for more than 90 million years. (Humans and chimpanzees, on the other hand, are more recently related.) Dolphins have adapted for life in the ocean. They sleep with half their brains awake to stay alert for sharks and other dangers. Despite their excellent eyesight, dolphins are primarily auditory creatures. They rely on a sense called echolocation to bounce rapid-fire clicking sounds off distant objects to read their shapes and positions. Dolphins will even eavesdrop on each other's echolocation signal to see—or, rather, hear—any fish or other goodies their friends are scanning. Can you imagine "hearing" your friend's sandwich? It all makes for a way of thinking much different from your own. "These animals live in a very different world," underwater photographer Brian Skerry says. "They're best described as an alien intelligence."

Burning Questions for These Chatty Animals ...

ELEPHANT TALK

Elephants speak to each other in a rumbling language that dips below the range of human hearing.

Burning question: Do you really never forget?

Humpback whales are the only whales that communicate through hauntingly beautiful songs as well as clicking sounds.

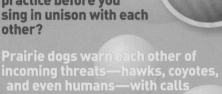
WHALE TALK

Burning question: Don't you need to practice before you sing in unison with each other?

Prairie dogs warn each other of incoming threats—hawks, coyotes, and even humans—with calls that are so detailed, they even describe the human's clothes and what he or she is carrying!

Burning question: What do you think of my outfit?

PRAIRIE DOG TALK

Could it Happen?

Deciphering dolphin speak is difficult for many reasons—not the least of which is their elusiveness. Although they're curious and will approach people, dolphins are fast swimmers who surface for air only every four minutes or so. "Studying dolphins is like studying an iceberg," says Kathleen Dudzinski, director of the Dolphin Communication Project, "because they spend most of their lives underwater." Researchers aren't even sure if dolphins have a language like English or Spanish: one made up of nouns and verbs. But that hasn't stopped scientists from teaching such concepts to captive dolphins using sign language and other systems. These dolphins have developed a quick grasp of not only simple commands such as fetch, but also "fetch the ball on the left side of the trainer."

Meanwhile, researchers are harnessing computers to record and analyze the ultra-fast clicks of dolphin language. Dolphin communication expert Denise Herzing has helped develop the C.H.A.T. system (short for "Cetacean Hearing and Telemetry"), an underwater device that translates English words into clicks that dolphins can understand. The system works with only a few words right now—"rope," "starfish," a piece of "sargassum" seaweed—but Herzing is hoping to decipher the basic units of dolphin language so we can someday all speak with dolphins, and perhaps even other animals, too. "I think that with all the new technology and software, we will be cracking the code of many species," says Herzing. "We will find that animals are encoding a lot of information in their signals. They are a lot smarter than we give them credit for."

DOLPHIN SIGN LANGUAGE

The Eyes Have it

What if you saw the world through the eyes of ...

... a human?

Well, this answer is obvious—it lies in plain sight! You see what you see because of the way your brain interprets visual signals transmitted from your peepers, which are packed with specialized cells and structures that focus the light bouncing off everything in view. Crucial to the process: special "photoreceptor" cells called rods and cones that line the tissue at the back of each eyeball. Rods process light and shadow; cones detect color. Human retinas contain three types of cone cells tuned to detect red, green, and blue light (people who are color-blind are missing cone cells for a particular color). Although eye structure varies wildly across the animal kingdom, scientists can often guess at how animals perceive their world by examining the types of photoreceptors in their eyes.

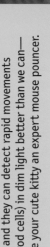

... a cat?

Cats have eight times as many rod cells as humans but far fewer cones, which means Mr. Whiskers is blind to some colors (reds and greens appear washed out) and unable to focus on objects farther away than 20 feet, or about six meters (cones capture fine details in addition to detecting colors). But all those rods bestow big benefits when it comes to stalking prey. Cats have extraordinary night vision (dusk to them is as clear as day), and they can detect rapid movements (another duty of rod cells) in dim light better than we can—abilities that make your cute kitty an expert mouse pouncer.

See next page for more!

... a dog?

Unlike humans, dogs have only two types of cone cells, meaning they are even more color-blind than cats (which have three types of cone cells). To a dog's eye, blues and yellows are vibrant; greens and reds are more like grays. Dogs suffer from the same nearsightedness as cats, but Spot is better at spotting motion at a distance. Dogs also have a wider field of view than both cats and humans and can see better in dim light than you—although cats are still champs at seeing in the dark.

... an eagle?

Imagine sitting in the cheap seats of a baseball stadium and being able to see the laces on the ball without using binoculars. Eagles have similar super-vision thanks to built-in telephoto lenses in each eye. Concentrations of cone cells in eagle eyes can focus on objects and animals—such as mice and fish—from hundreds of feet in the air. Eagles and other birds such as chickens have a fourth type of photoreceptor that humans lack, enabling them to see colors—including vibrantly purple ultraviolet colors—that you can't. Researchers think birds developed their exceptional color perception and motion-detection vision for hunting in broad daylight.

What if you saw the world through the eyes of …

… a giant squid?

The basketball-size eyes of this deep-sea monster are the largest in the animal kingdom for a reason: They're supremely adapted for life in the gloomy depths. Pupils as big as oranges capture every last bit of light, including the faint flashes cast by glow-in-the-dark deep-sea creatures when they're batted aside by larger animals (such as sperm whales: both predator and prey of the giant squid). Meanwhile, headlight-like organs inside each of the squid's eyeballs cast a faint glow to help the squid latch on to nearby targets. Giant squids are almost certainly color-blind, but then color vision is hardly helpful in their nearly pitch-black realm.

… a jumping spider?

You would have eyes on the back of your head! Jumping spiders have eight eyes that offer a 360-degree view of their world: two primary eyes facing front, two pairs on each side of their heads, and a pair facing backward. But not all of these peepers see the same. The two primary eyes detect color just like human eyes (researchers have learned that jumping spiders will even watch TV), while the six stationary eyes are more for spotting motion rather than detail. Such supreme peripheral vision helps these fearsome hunters detect threats or lock on to prey before pouncing up to 50 times the length of their bodies.

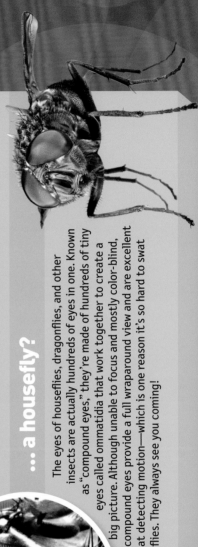

... a mantis shrimp?

Equipped with nature's most mysterious peepers, this foot-long (30-cm) crustacean sees the world in a whole new light. Actually, "see" isn't quite the right word here. While humans have three types of color-detecting photoreceptors, the mantis shrimp has 12 of them, set in compound eyes atop stalks that can point in any direction. The shrimp's stalks "scan" the creature's coral-reef habitat to create an instant image of color, vibrant ultraviolet light, and even shimmering polarized light without bothering to process the signals like the human brain does. This instant-imaging system helps the shrimp lash out at prey with its lightning-quick arms—among the fastest in the animal kingdom.

... a housefly?

The eyes of houseflies, dragonflies, and other insects are actually hundreds of eyes in one. Known as "compound eyes," they're made of hundreds of tiny eyes called ommatidia that work together to create a big picture. Although unable to focus and mostly color-blind, compound eyes provide a full wraparound view and are excellent at detecting motion—which is one reason it's so hard to swat flies. They always see you coming!

What if

Today Sasquatch. Tomorrow, the Loch Ness monster?

The creature emerged from the shadows of the moonlit forest, its eyes glowing yellow in the two campers' flashlight beam. The startled pair suddenly found themselves face-to-waist with the shaggy nine-foot (2.7-m)-tall beast known as Bigfoot, the legendary apelike creature said to wander the wilderness of the Pacific Northwest and elsewhere. Also known as Sasquatch (a term based on a Native American name for the many wild men of North American folklore), Bigfoot has been the subject of more than 3,000 such eyewitness accounts going back centuries. Roughly 10,000 of the creature's tracks—most at least 14 inches (36 cm) long—have been reported since the 1800s. But despite all the sightings, no one has uncovered conclusive evidence of Bigfoot: dead or alive. How would the discovery of a genuine specimen change the world?

Body of Evidence

Bigfoot true believers insist that Bigfoot could be a surviving member of a long-extinct species, such as *Gigantopithecus* (an oversize ape that disappeared 100,000 years ago), a Neanderthal early human, or some previously undiscovered member of the great ape family that includes gorillas and chimpanzees. If Bigfoot seekers confirmed any of these theories— by finding a live *Gigantopithecus*, for instance—the media would go ape over the discovery. Bigfoot would no longer lurk in the back pages of tabloid newspapers; it would become the front-page attraction of every major newspaper, the lead story of every website. Sasquatch would become such a star that it would need protection. Cryptozoologists (or people who study legendary creatures) estimate that fewer than 6,000 of these shaggy beasts lurk in the wild, making it an endangered species. Laws would be passed to protect Bigfoot. Park rangers would patrol its habitat.

And while news shows would scramble for Sasquatch interviews and sneaker companies would pay Bigfoot big bucks to endorse size-20 athletic shoes, scientists would make the biggest deal out of the discovery. Evidence of a surviving population of apes or early humans from the distant past—a so-called relict hominoid—would fill in the gaps of our evolutionary family tree and lend credence to the existence of similar legendary creatures. "There were multiple species of hominoids [apes and early humans] coexisting across the landscape throughout the past—sometimes as many as half a dozen," says Idaho State University anthropologist Dr. Jeffrey Meldrum. "The hominoid family tree is ever 'bushier,' and it is becoming evident that many of these branches persisted until very recently." Discovery of a single Bigfoot specimen, living or dead, would reenergize the search for other relict species that might be hiding in remote corners of the globe. In a world where Bigfoot is real, after all, could the Yeti of the Himalaya or even the skunk ape of the Florida Everglades be the next big discovery?

What if these legends were legit?

Unicorns?

UNICORN

The good news: According to myth, these one-horned horses had magical healing abilities.

The bad news: Unfortunately, the only way to obtain these healing abilities was to grind up a unicorn's horn.

Closest contender: The Siberian rhinoceros—a shaggy rhino that lived alongside humans as recently as 29,000 years ago—is one of several horned animals thought to have inspired the earliest unicorn legends.

Mermaids?

The good news: Mermaids have the power to calm rough seas and grant underwater-breathing abilities.

The bad news: In Greek legends, mermaids use their beauty and sweet singing abilities to lure sailors to their doom.

Closest contender: Noting that they were "not half as beautiful as they are painted," Christopher Columbus spotted three "mermaids" while sailing for the New World in 1493. Turns out they were manatees, marine mammals occasionally mistaken for mermaids by sailors who've clearly been too long at sea.

MERMAID

Could it Happen?

In 2008, a binocular company offered a million bucks to anyone who could prove Bigfoot's existence. The cash went unclaimed. And despite decades of Bigfoot hunting, no one has recovered a body of the beast—a fact often cited by skeptics as proof that Bigfoot is bogus. Yet true believers point to samples of supposed Sasquatch fur that don't match any known animal. They replay controversial 1967 film footage of an apelike creature striding through the Northern California wilderness while peering creepily over its shoulder at the cameraman. And they follow the footprints, some of which show evidence of something called a "midtarsal break," a variation from the human foot that allows greater flexibility in the mid-sole area. "It indicates an adaptation that is distinct but elegantly appropriate for a large bipedal primate in a rugged steep terrain," says Dr. Meldrum. But with civilization spreading so far and so fast, surely we would have found at least one of the 6,000 or so nine-foot (2.7-m)-tall shaggy beasts allegedly roaming the Pacific Northwest. Tell that to the scientists who found the previously uncounted 125,000 lowland gorillas in Central Africa in 2008. For Bigfoot believers, the wilderness is still big enough for Sasquatch to hide!

BIGFOOT PRINT

What if
you were raised by wolves ?

Start wagging that tail. Life in a wolf pack is fun— and a lot like home!

Sometimes Dad might turn into a papa bear if he gets up too early on a Saturday morning, or maybe Mom acts like a silly goose when she stays up too late. But at least your parents aren't complete animals! The idea of children raised by wolves (and apes, deer, and even birds) is a common theme in books, movies, and mythology. What if you were adopted by a pack of wolves—say gray wolves, for instance, the most common species—in real life? The good news is you'll get to howl at the moon. The bad news is you'll still have plenty of chores. And Mom and Dad won't take no for an answer.

and the older wolves are out hunting, you'll stay home to babysit the youngest, rowdiest pups at the rendezvous site. Work on your stalking skills and someday you'll get the ickiest chore of all: delivery dog. It'll be your job to spit up food for the pups after returning from a kill, letting them lick your face for leftovers. Maybe you should convince the pack to order pizza instead.

Top Dogs

Your parents call the shots at home. It's no different in a wolf pack! The mom and dad wolf are the strongest and wisest of the group, in charge of keeping the family safe and putting meat in everyone's bellies. "A wolf pack is a family: a mother, a father, and their offspring," says wolf expert L. David Mech. Just like members of a human family, wolves in a pack cooperate, play, squabble, and talk to each other. Younger members—offspring from previous years—heed their elders and learn life lessons in hunting and raising young. Once they're a year old, pack wolves are expected to lend a helping paw. "Yearlings look after the pups and play with them," says wolf researcher Barbara Molnar, "just as older siblings do in a human family."

As a member of the pack, you'll have chores to do and roles to play (being a human won't get you out of them). Sometimes you'll need to stand guard while everyone sleeps and bark an alarm when trouble approaches. While Mom, Dad,

WOLF CUB

Side Effects Include ...

PACK RAP

Your human mom might get mad when you slouch, but sloppy posture is the highest form of respect in the wolf world. Younger wolves crouch and tuck their tails around pack leaders. Happy wolves wag their tails and give a playful bow just like domestic dogs. Unhappy wolves are even easier to read. Has your dad ever shot you a stern glance when you did something wrong? Father and mother wolves do the same thing with unruly offspring.

WOLF PACK

NON-SCENTS

Catching a whiff of a stinky sibling is never nice. To members of a wolf family, however, odor is just another way to communicate. Using urine or the pads of its paws, a wolf will mark the family's territory and transmit info about his or her identity, including age, social status, and much more. Your wolf siblings' sense of smell is a hundred times more sensitive than your own, so you'll just need to play along.

CATCHING A SCENT

HOWL ARE YOU?

Nothing builds team spirit in the pack quite like a good group howl. Wolves howl in a chorus often: when they wake up, before a hunt, perhaps even for fun. Audible up to 10 miles (16 km) away in the right terrain, a howl also functions as the pack's long-distance phone service. Wolves will howl to call members to a rendezvous site, warn of danger to the pups, or tell neighboring packs to keep off their land.

HOWLING

Could it Happen?

The orphan boy Mowgli is raised by wolves in Disney's *The Jungle Book*. Same goes for the twin brothers Romulus and Remus in Roman mythology. But these are just stories and fairy tales. Wild animals could never actually raise a human child, right? After all, compared to animal offspring that can hop to their feet just minutes after entering the world, human babies are helpless for the first few years of life. Believe it or not, history is full of about a hundred allegedly true tales of wild animals raising orphaned children—so-called feral children. Take, for instance, Russia's Oxana Malaya, who as a girl was discovered living with a pack of dogs until she was eight years old. (They provided her with warmth and scraps of meat.) Malaya readjusted to life as a human, but she could still switch back to doglike behavior—panting, barking, and running on all fours—even in her twenties. Such tales, although often difficult to verify, are tinged with sadness, typically the result of parental neglect. So even though life with a pack of wolves might sound like a howling good time, remember: There's no place like home.

Chapter 4:

TiME WaRpED

Imagine waking up in a world where Christopher Columbus never landed in the Americas, everyone on Earth spoke the same language, and you were stuck in a dead-end job of high-seas piracy (the key word here: "dead"). Get ready to witness the past get blasted into alternate timelines, where famous figures and momentous events zigged instead of zagged. History class was never like this!

What if Neanderthals never went extinct?

What Would Happen if...

What if

Throw some burgers on the grill. Your closest evolutionary relatives are coming to dinner.

It's a murder mystery more than 50,000 years old. Two men faced off in a cave in what is now northern Iraq, and only one man walked away. The victim was a Neanderthal, a type of early human, killed by a spear to the chest. His murderer may have been a *Homo sapien,* aka a modern human, a member of our own species and one of your ancestors. The evidence is the trace of the murder weapon itself. Scientists studying the Neanderthal man's body— discovered in an Iraqi cave in the 1950s—found a rib injury matching the sorts of spears hurled in special slings by prehistoric modern humans. In the face of such advanced weapons technology, the Neanderthals didn't stand a chance. Within 10,000 years, not a single Neanderthal was left on Earth. Conflict with *Homo sapiens* is one suspected cause of their disappearance. But what if they had survived long enough to order cheeseburgers and trade their cave dwellings for apartment buildings?

DID EARLY MAN CAUSE THE DOWNFALL OF NEANDERTHALS?

Same but Different

As you'd expect from our closest evolutionary relatives, Neanderthals shared many similarities with modern humans. Scientists suspect they wore clothes, wielded tools, harnessed fire for cooking and warmth, buried their dead, chatted using simple language, and perhaps even expressed their creative sides by carving images into cave walls. But while we *Homo sapiens* thrived because of our ability to adapt to new situations and environments, Neanderthals mainly specialized in one activity: hunting hulking Ice Age animals, such as woolly rhinos, horses, and reindeer. Even as our *Homo sapiens* ancestors invented nets and other tools to catch rabbits, turtles, and other smaller morsels of protein, Neanderthals stuck to stalking big game.

This sort of rigid way of life—this specialization—could carry over into any Neanderthal group

that survived to today. Less adept at adapting, they would likely find it hard to fit in with *Homo sapiens* culture. Instead of smartphones and social media, modern-day Neanderthals might stick with face-to-face communication in their own closely knit communities. "We live in such a social world," says Briana Pobiner, a prehistoric anthropologist at the Smithsonian National Museum of Natural History, "and Neanderthals may have lacked the ability for that sophisticated communication—an ability to imagine the future and talk about the past." Modern-day Neanderthals would probably be the strong, silent types, which would leave us in a world inhabited by two separate intelligent species living in isolation from each other—and hopefully free of any fights like the one in that Iraqi cave 50,000 years ago.

Side Effects Include ...

COLD WARRIORS

With stockier bodies to help retain heat and broader noses to warm the air they breathed, Neanderthals were well suited for life in an Ice Age environment. Modern members of their species would likely stick to communities and careers in the coldest corners of the globe. They would make great snowboarding instructors but lousy surf teachers. In fact, tropical environments would be tortuously scorching without air-conditioning.

BUILT FOR THE ICE AGE

FEARSOME FEATURES

BIG BROWS

Wherever they traveled in *Homo sapiens* society, Neanderthals would stick out in a crowd. They had prominent brows above large eyes, football-shaped skulls, stocky bodies, stumpy fingers, small chins, and fat noses. Some Neanderthals also had freckles and red hair. They were physically stronger than *Homo sapiens*, and scientists now suspect they possessed dexterity nearly on par with modern humans. A Neanderthal handling a smartphone wouldn't necessarily be all thumbs.

MEAT ELITES

Homo sapiens thrived while Neanderthals died in large part because we were less picky with what we put in our mouths. We added plants to our plates and processed wheat into bread until we achieved the culinary perfection of the pepperoni pizza. Neanderthals stuck with mammoth steaks and rhino kabobs flame broiled over a roaring fire. If they had carried on with their cookouts until modern times, today's Neanderthal-owned restaurants would probably offer the biggest barbecue bison burger you could find.

HUNTING

Could it Happen?

Before they went extinct, Neanderthals had spread into Europe, Central Asia, and the Middle East more than 100,000 years before we *Homo sapiens* began our migration from Africa. Although the reasons for the Neanderthals' extinction are largely a mystery, competition with modern humans was likely a major factor. If a community of these cave dwellers had managed to find an isolated spot where they could hide out and ride out the ice ages, we would have Neanderthal neighbors in the far north today. "They might have ended up like modern humans who make a living in Siberia hunting for reindeer," Pobiner says. Over time, this group of early humans may have learned some lessons from modern humans—such as using nets to capture smaller animals. They might have even learned to play nice with *Homo sapiens*. "If fitting in with another species was important to their survival," Pobiner says, "they could have figured it out after coexisting for another 40,000 years. But these Neanderthals would be so much different from anything we humans have interacted with."

In some small way, Neanderthals *have* survived to today. Scientists have genetic evidence that early humans and modern humans mingled tens of thousands of years ago. Any humans today whose ancestors interbred with Neanderthals carry a bit of cave-dweller DNA.

What if

It might be easier to get some things done, but life wouldn't be as fun.

Human beings didn't invent the idea of shaping sounds into words to communicate thoughts. Researchers suspect that our evolutionary ancestors began inventing words to describe tools and fire-making techniques as far back as a million years ago, long before our species—*Homo sapiens*—appeared on the fossil record. No doubt the first *Homo sapiens* added to the conversation when they first appeared 200,000 years ago. But as they spread from Africa to populate Asia, Europe, and eventually the rest of the world around 55,000 years ago, our ancestors began to develop more complicated tools—and the words to describe them—in isolation of each other. The farther these pockets of humanity moved from southwestern Africa, the more their languages changed. And that's why we have more than 6,500 languages spoken around the world today. But what if all those tongues were tied into one common language for everyone?

Loss for **Words**

A world with only a single language might seem like an easier place to live. And in certain situations where communication is crucial—radio chatter in the airline industry, for example—everyone involved agrees to speak the same language to avoid dangerous misunderstandings. If every citizen spoke a common tongue in every country on Earth, international trade, banking, travel, and asking directions to the nearest bathroom would be a snap.

But language is more than just a system of grammar and vocabulary. It's intertwined with the speakers' culture, history, and distinctiveness: their stories and songs, customs and laws, fashions and flavors. That's why any foreign-language class involves more than just memorizing vocabulary on flash cards. It's a lesson in history and culture, too. Only about a third of the world's languages have a written component—a way to record culture and history over the long term. Settling on a common tongue would wipe the slate clean for thousands of cultures. Styles would merge. Stories would start to sound the same. Flavors would blend together. "We would lose other ways of looking at the world," says language expert Allan Metcalf.

Side Effects Include ...

SAY WHAT?

Speaking the same language wouldn't guarantee that everyone would understand each other. Accents and dialects—regional variations in vocabulary—would still trip up conversations and lead to some hilariously awkward misunderstandings. "The word [for] 'bread,' for example, means different things in different parts of the world," says Metcalf. "Consider the differences between British and American English. There are entire books about it."

BAD MEDICINE

Communities that live close to nature—such as Native Americans and forest-dwelling tribes in Southeast Asia—have a much more specialized vocabulary for types of soil and plants, and this expertise has helped scientists discover a wide range of medicines, from treatments for diabetes to the wonder-drug aspirin. If these smaller communities abandoned their language for a universal one, scientists would lose a wealth of information about plants that could be harvested into life-saving medicines.

WAR OF THE WORDS

Even if the world's population did settle on a common tongue, chances are it wouldn't stay the primary language for long. A language's popularity rides on the fortunes of the nations where it is spoken. If learning a different language will suddenly help a group of people improve their quality of life, they will make the switch. It gives new meaning to the expression "money talks." "In the past, Latin was [the common language] throughout Europe for clergy and scholars," says Metcalf, "and there was a time when French was the world's diplomatic language. Now English goes almost everywhere, but as a second language."

BREAD

CURRENCY

Could it Happen?

If you were to invite all seven billion or so people in the world to a picnic, you'd have a tougher time finding enough potato salad than universal translators. Although the world's population speaks thousands of languages, a staggering 75 percent of people speak the 85 most common ones. And the lesser used tongues are going extinct at a rate of about one every four months. Nearly half the world's languages may be forgotten in a hundred years as small communities adopt the world's more commonly spoken languages: Chinese, Spanish, English, Hindi, and Arabic. But these top five are too entrenched to fade in favor of one clear common language. "Even if we had just one common language," says Metcalf, "it would soon split up, because any living language adjusts itself to accommodate the new situations that always arise." Which puts us back to where we started in Africa, when our ancestors began wandering the world, inventing new words as they went.

What if you had a time machine ?

Get ready for the trip of several lifetimes!

You don't need some fancy vehicle to travel through time. You're doing it right now, plowing forward through the decades at a rate of one second for every second. And according to laws of physics first theorized by Albert Einstein and later proved by observations and experiments, time slows down for you (relative to everyone else) as you speed up. This "time dilation" will pose a problem for astronauts who return home from deep-space missions to find their friends and loved ones have reached old age, but for this scenario you're going to travel in the opposite direction: to the past. Please keep your hands and feet inside the time machine as we rewind Earth's history.

FIRST STOP: A.D. 1700
New York City, North America, 11:10 a.m.

Today, New York City is the largest metropolis in the United States and home to more than eight million people. In 1700, less than 75 years after Dutch colonists built a seaside trading post named New Amsterdam on the tip of the island of Manhattan, only about 5,000 people lived here. You don't see any of the city's famous skyscrapers as you stroll along its few paved streets—including Wall Street, named for an actual wall that until recently ran alongside it. You spy only some clapboard houses and squat stone buildings. Near the wharfs, you see sunburned sailors dressed in colorful jackets with flintlock pistols jammed in their belts. Pirates! At this point in history, New York City was North America's most popular port for these bandits of the high seas. You decide you'd rather not mingle with these mean-looking fellows. Time to leave!

SECOND STOP: A.D. 1360
Warwick Castle, England, 2:40 p.m.

You're surprised to see that the walls and towers of this English castle are painted a brilliant white rather than the drab gray of today's castle ruins. The lord and lady are proud of their stone home and have had the walls whitewashed. They lavish even more attention on their interior décor. Chamber walls are paneled with wood and hung with elaborate cloth paintings (which help block frigid drafts). Although the keep's lower floors are dim, damp, and chilly, the upper levels have large windows with spectacular views of the surrounding countryside. The great hall, where the lord and lady entertain and hold court, reverberates with revelry. You've arrived on the day of a holiday feast! The kitchen's cooks pull out all their culinary tricks, preparing heaping dishes smothered in rich sauces and coated with imported spices. Fancy a peacock cooked in its feathers? How about a roasted porpoise or seal? Maybe you have a taste for fried stork? Grab it to go. It's time to zip to your next destination.

WARWICK CASTLE, ENGLAND

HISTORIC MAP OF MANHATTAN

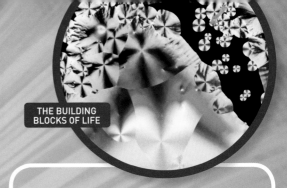
THE BUILDING
BLOCKS OF LIFE

THIRD STOP: 1100 B.C.
Deir el-Medina, ancient Egypt, 12:03 p.m.

The noon sun beats down mercilessly as you walk the dusty streets of this walled village in ancient Egypt. You must be here on a weekend, because the narrow streets are bustling with artisans who've returned from their work crafting tombs and treasures for the rich and powerful in the nearby Valley of the Kings. You hear two neighbors argue over the price of some fish. Money hasn't been invented yet, so buyers barter with sellers to figure out fair trades. Soft singing wafts from a nearby rooftop as you head indoors to beat the heat. Like most Egyptian homes, the houses in Deir el-Medina have just four or so dimly lit rooms and maybe a basement to store valuables. Wood is scarce in the kingdom, so houses are furnished with just a few low stools and chests, plus a brick platform for the bed. What are these shards of pottery piled near the family goat? They're letters! One shard is a laundry list. Another tells a ghost story. The last is from a schoolteacher. "Bring your chapter and come!" it says. You scribble a response just for fun: "I will do it!" Archaeologists will find your letter in about 3,000 years.

DEIR EL-MEDINA

FINAL STOP: 3.8 BILLION B.C.
unnamed island, 8:14 a.m.

You park your time machine on a tiny island in a shallow globe-spanning soup of chemicals: amino acids and fats, the basic components of life. Whatever you do, don't roll down the window or step outside. This early Earth is not the blue-and-green marble we marvel at in the 21st century. Liquid water is the hot new thing (literally—it's extremely hot) and continents don't exist yet. The air is a toxic fog of vicious vapors: carbon monoxide, carbon dioxide, nitrogen, methane, cyanide. A lightning strike jolts the chemical soup offshore of your island. Perhaps it sparked the formation of the first life-forms, simple single-celled microscopic bacteria. You can't see these organisms with the naked eye, but you snap a smartphone pic and set a course back to the future. Your friends in the 21st century aren't going to believe this!

FOURTH STOP: 240 MILLION B.C.
Pangaea supercontinent, 4:50 p.m.

This is not Earth as you know it today. All of the planet's continents—or landmasses—have joined into one supercontinent known as Pangaea. The hot, dry interior here is a paradise for reptiles, which have been growing in size. You spot the first dinosaur, a creature no larger than a kangaroo, munching on plant leaves. You set your time machine to fast forward to see what happens next. Twenty million years pass in the blink of an eye as dinosaurs explode in diversity around you. Pangaea begins to break up and spread these creatures to every continent on Earth. They will reign for nearly 150 million years until an asteroid impact wipes out all the non-bird species of dinosaur. You definitely don't want to stick around for that.

PETRIFIED FOREST
NATIONAL PARK

What if

You'd have to travel the world for a bowl of spaghetti.

The ocean was indeed blue—and the seas calm—when Italian explorer Christopher Columbus set sail on his famous voyage of discovery in the name of Spain in 1492. The storms came later: first of the ship-wrecking sort and eventually in a hurricane of controversy. It turns out Columbus wasn't the first European to set foot in the Americas (historians believe a Viking named Leif Eriksson voyaged from Greenland to the northern tip of Newfoundland, Canada, around A.D. 1000). In fact, Columbus didn't even set foot in North America at all. He landed in the Bahamas—and that was by accident. Although he was a skilled navigator, Columbus mistook these islands for Asia after underestimating the circumference of the Earth in his quest for a trade route to the other side of the world. But despite Columbus's stumbles, his arrival in the "New World" of the Americas was a momentous historical event. What if Columbus hadn't sailed the ocean blue in 1492?

Bridge Toll

Despite what old history books might say, Christopher Columbus didn't "discover" the New World. People already lived there, after all (the first humans began crossing into North America from Asia at least 15,000 years ago). It was Columbus's interactions with these residents that changed history. Historians call these interactions the "Columbian Exchange": a sharing of technology and crops, animals and weapons, ideas and even diseases between the Old World of Europe, Asia, and Africa and the New World of the Americas. Think of it as a bridge of ships over the Atlantic Ocean.

No one living in the Americas had seen a horse until Columbus brought them on his second voyage. As horses spread across North America, they eventually revolutionized how Native Americans hunted and got around. No Native Americans had seen cattle and chickens, pigs and pet cats until European explorers ferried them from the Old World. Columbus and later explorers, meanwhile, returned home with turkeys, ducks, llamas, and other fascinating animals from the New World. The grapes, olives, peaches, and honey you eat in North America today were all transplants from the Old World, which in return received potatoes, corn, tomatoes, and other hearty foods from North America. If Columbus hadn't landed in the Americas—and if he hadn't been followed by any other Old World explorers until much later in history—this exchange of animals, ideas, and technology would have been much delayed. But the Columbian Exchange wasn't mutually beneficial for people on both sides of the Atlantic Ocean, as you're about to see ...

Side Effects Include ...

PAST INTENSE

GOLD

European explorers raided the New World for gold. In exchange, they brought a deadly import. Smallpox, chicken pox, and other diseases carried from the Old World wiped out more than half of the Native Americans, who had no immunity. The deaths of powerful Inca and Aztec kings weakened these vibrant cultures, which were both virtually gone within 40 years of Columbus's landing. Without diseases brought by the Columbian Exchange, these civilizations may have continued to thrive.

POPULATION EXPLOSION

POTATOES

Old World oxen and other big beasts of burden revolutionized farming in the Americas, while New World crops such as potatoes, sweet potatoes, corn, and tomatoes provided an easier source of food for the starving people of Europe. Soon, the world population more than doubled because everyone had more to eat. Without the Columbian Exchange, populations on both sides of the Atlantic would have stayed leaner and lighter.

CHANGING TIDES

Columbus claimed the New World for Spain, which exploited its riches to become a global superpower rivaled only by Portugal. If an explorer from England, France, the Netherlands, or China had reached the New World first, any of those countries would likely have become a dominant force in the world much more quickly. The result: Today's maps and history books would look a lot different!

COLUMBUS LANDS IN THE NEW WORLD

Could it Happen?

It was just blind luck that Christopher Columbus had smooth sailing during his historic voyage in 1492. He had launched his fleet during hurricane season long before mariners could track such massive storms with even primitive instruments. (Columbus lost one of his ships to a hurricane on a later voyage.) But even if Columbus had gotten lost at sea, turned back early, or never secured funding for his trip at all, chances are that the New World wouldn't have remained "undiscovered" for long. "It's clear that some European would have made landfall in the Americas not long after 1492," says historian Edward Tenner. The search for a trade route across the Atlantic was intense, and the so-called age of discovery was in full swing. Just eight years after Columbus set sail, a Portuguese explorer named Pedro Álvares Cabral was blown off course while sailing along the west coast of Africa. His crew began seeing seaweed, birds, and other signs that a coast was near. The next day, they spotted land. Cabral made landfall in Brazil and claimed it for Portugal, one of the world's largest superpowers at the time. If Columbus hadn't set sail, the history of the New World would likely have followed a similar course, perhaps with a Cabralian Exchange instead of a Columbian one.

PEDRO ÁLVARES CABRAL

What if

A lot more Americans might be speaking French or Spanish today.

Crowds cheered and cannons boomed across New Orleans on December 20, 1803, as the French flag lowered slowly in the main square and a new flag—this one with stars—rose in its place. The United States had recently doubled its size with the Louisiana Purchase, one of the largest property sales in history. This big deal included much more than the vital port city of New Orleans. It extended west of the Mississippi River to the Rocky Mountains and north from the Gulf of Mexico to Canada. The U.S. government bought the Louisiana territory—all 828,000 square miles (2.1 million sq km) of it—from France for the price of $15 million, or about four cents an acre. More than just one of the biggest bargains in real estate history, this transaction changed the course of the United States—and the world. But what if this good buy had gone goodbye?

STATUE OF ANDREW JACKSON AT THE SAINT LOUIS CATHEDRAL

Land of the Free (for Cheap)

U.S. president Thomas Jefferson believed the Louisiana territory would be a wilderness filled with wonders, from woolly mammoths to towering volcanoes. Explorers to the west found wonders of a different sort: a land rich in gold and silver, forests ripe with timber for building, and endless plains that might eventually make good farmland. At least parts or all of 15 states were eventually formed from the Louisiana territory. It also gave the United States control of its first superhighway, the Mississippi River. A vital route for shipping and sharing information, the Mississippi unified the country.

Historians consider the Louisiana Purchase one of America's defining moments, right up with the creation of the U.S. Declaration of Independence and the Constitution.

THOMAS JEFFERSON

All of the territory's resources—and all that living space—transformed the United States from a fledgling republic into a superpower that became a beacon of freedom and democracy for other parts of the world. If the deal had died, anyone born west of the Mississippi today might be citizens of France, Spain, or Mexico, speaking French or Spanish as their native language (similar to how many citizens of Canada speak French today). "It could easily have wound up a French or Spanish territory," says historian Charles C. Bolton. Americans wanting to visit natural wonders such as Yellowstone and the Grand Canyon would need to leave the United States. Or perhaps not. If France had never sold the Louisiana territory to the United States to begin with, the two countries likely would have battled over it later.

Side Effects Include ...

RAW DEAL

The Louisiana Purchase only increased the U.S. government's appetite for land. By the middle of the 19th century, Americans believed they had a destiny to expand the country from coast to coast—regardless of who was in the way. Native Americans, who lived here first, were pushed off their sacred lands and forced to live on reservations, harsh areas stricken by disease and poverty. Overhunting by settlers left them without food, forcing them to depend on the U.S. government for help.

ORIGINAL RESIDENTS

ALTERED STATES

The country's sudden growth spurt sent shock waves through history. States that supported the practice of slavery had maintained a careful balance with the states that opposed it. But soon new states began establishing themselves out West, which became a political battleground over slavery as more and more Americans opposed the spread of slavery from the South. Eventually, the conflicts reached a head in the American Civil War, which brought about an end to slavery in 1865.

COURSE CLOSED

Without the Louisiana Purchase, President Jefferson wouldn't have authorized the greatest cross-country hike in history, dispatching his secretary Captain Meriwether Lewis and Lewis's friend William Clark to chart the new Louisiana territory. Lewis and Clark led more than 30 rugged outdoorsmen (and one teenage girl, Native American guide Sacagawea) along the Missouri River, across the treacherous Rocky Mountains, and all the way to the Pacific Ocean before heading home.

LEWIS AND CLARK

Could it Happen?

NAPOLEON BONAPARTE

The Louisiana Purchase was like one of those Black Friday sales right after Thanksgiving: a great deal for a limited time only. Possession of the Louisiana territory had bounced between France and Spain ever since the land was claimed for France's King Louis XIV (hence the name "Louisiana") by a French explorer in 1682. By 1803, it was back in France's hands. But French Emperor Napoleon Bonaparte needed fast cash to wage war against his nation's chief rival, England, which he also hoped to throw off balance by helping its former colony double in size. Thomas Jefferson was interested only in buying New Orleans and access to the Gulf of Mexico; Bonaparte shocked America by offering much more—a deal Jefferson couldn't refuse.

Still, this sale of the centuries faced opposition from Americans who thought Jefferson was overstepping his authority under the Constitution. The treasury didn't even have enough money to cover the price. (The United States had to borrow from European banks to close the deal.) If Jefferson hadn't pushed hard for the purchase, Bonaparte might have bid adieu. The sale launched the countries on two different trajectories: America became a superpower; Bonaparte suffered a crushing defeat to England 12 years later.

What if

the South had won the American Civil War?

The effects on history might reach all the way to the moon!

The bombardment began early one spring morning in 1861, a storm of explosives that rained down on the island holdfast of Fort Sumter in Charleston, South Carolina, U.S.A. The newly formed Confederate States Army of the southern states had just fired the opening salvo against the Union Army of the northern states in the American Civil War, which would rage over the next four years and cost more than 700,000 lives. The stakes couldn't have been higher. The war was fought over many things including the rights of the southern states—which called themselves the Confederate States of America—to keep slaves, a crucial component of the South's economy. When the Civil War ended on April 9, 1865, with the Confederacy's surrender to the North, the slaves in the rebelling states had already been declared free by President Abraham Lincoln's Emancipation Proclamation in 1865. The 13th Amendment to the Constitution was ratified at the end of the year, outlawing slavery for good. Nearly four million former slaves were suddenly free. But what if the war had gone the other way?

CIVIL WAR REENACTMENT

Emancipation's Proclamation

EMANCIPATION PROCLAMATION

The Civil War may have started in 1861, but the tensions leading up to it had been simmering for more than a decade over the institution of slavery and its expansion beyond the South. In 1857, the United States Supreme Court decided that black people were not citizens with the same rights as white people, and that the U.S. government had no power to regulate slavery in the country's new territories. A lawyer and politician named Abraham Lincoln questioned the decision. He ran for president in 1860 and won. People in the South—who despised Lincoln for his antislavery views—saw his election as a threat to their way of life. Southern states soon began seceding from (or leaving) the Union. The Confederate States of America (C.S.A.) was born.

In a world where the South came out on top, the Confederacy would have retained its independence from the United States. "They saw themselves in many ways as the true inheritors of the legacy of the American Revolution," says historian Charles C. Bolton, "and that their rights were being usurped by the North, who was trying to take away their property." The C.S.A. already had its own president,

currency, capital, and constitution that protected slavery. Neither Lincoln's Emancipation Proclamation nor the 13th Amendment to the U.S. Constitution would have applied to what was essentially a separate nation.

Slavery would have undoubtedly continued in the South, but for how long? "The system of slavery was already under a lot of stress by the 1850s as increasing numbers of slaves escaped to the North," Bolton says, "but I think it would have persisted for a fair amount of time because cotton cultivation required physical labor." Machines for picking cotton weren't perfected until the 1930s, and that means slavery on the cotton plantations would have likely continued until at least the 20th century. "We would like to think it would have died out pretty quickly," says Bolton, "but sadly that's not likely the case. Slavery was just too important to the South's economy."

Misfortunes of War: The Challenges Facing a Victorious South

The Civil War left the South's cotton-based economy in ruins. "So much of their capital was invested in human beings," says Bolton, "and that capital was wiped out in an instant with the emancipation of the slaves." But even if the South had won, its economy would have faced many trials, including ...

... cotton competition: The South's hold on the cotton market began slipping during the war, when the northern states and other countries began to import cotton from Egypt and India. After the war, the South would need every advantage—including its use of slave labor—to compete in the global cotton market.

COTTON

... the future: While the South's economy depended heavily on farming, the North was embracing industrialization (or the manufacturing of goods in factories). "It was moving in line with where the world was moving," says Bolton, "toward economic prosperity." Shifting toward industrialization would have been difficult in the South, where white workers would have resented losing out on jobs to slaves.

... cash crisis: You might think that everyone in the North opposed slavery. Not the case! "Northern financial institutions financed the southern plantation economy," says Bolton. "So after the war, the South would have to develop those institutions all on their own."

See next page for more!

Southern Segregation

History provides some clues for how slavery might have eventually ended in a victorious Confederacy. Even though the North won the Civil War in 1865, black Americans still faced terrible treatment. Despite a series of amendments to the U.S. Constitution guaranteeing black people citizenship and the right to vote, a system of segregation began taking shape in the late 1800s. In the South, Jim Crow laws restricted black people to their own restaurants and restrooms, schools, pools, beaches, and churches. These places were supposed to be "separate but equal" but rarely were. Segregation was the shadow of slavery, a way to keep black people in poverty and under the control of a ruling class of white people.

It endured until the civil rights movement of the 1950s and '60s, when black people stood up for their right to receive equal treatment despite attacks from terrorist groups such as the Ku Klux Klan and brutal treatment from the police. Newspaper and TV coverage of young and old protesters blasted by fire hoses and bitten by police dogs shocked the nation and world, which led to the passing of the Civil Rights Act in 1964. It outlawed discrimination and racial segregation in schools and at the workplace.

Although slavery was still going strong in parts of South America and Africa into the late 1800s, much of the world saw it for what it was: an evil that needed to be eliminated. Just as black people in the 1950s stood up for their rights, slaves in a victorious South would have likely done the same. Their battle for equality would've been even more dangerous. Slaves were human property in society built on controlling them, after all. But given time and prompted by heroic—and no doubt bloody—antislavery demonstrations in a world connected by media, international scrutiny and economic penalties would eventually lead to the downfall of slavery in the South.

Side Effects Include ...

LINCOLN LIVES

President Abraham Lincoln had seen the country through its darkest time and helped preserve it, but the Civil War made him many enemies. Less than a week after the South's surrender, a Confederate sympathizer fatally shot the president at close range. Freed black people, along with many white Northerners, lined the streets of his funeral parade to pay their respects to the "Great Emancipator." If the North had lost, Lincoln likely wouldn't have been assassinated, and the fractured nation would have benefited from his wisdom.

ABRAHAM LINCOLN

SUPERPOWER FAILURE

After the Civil War, the Northern government began a reconstruction effort to welcome the war-shattered South back into the Union. Despite much resentment in the former Confederate States of America, the United States became whole again and developed into a superpower, able to affect events on a global scale. But if the South had won the war, the U.S.A. and the C.S.A. would have remained two separate squabbling nations instead of a single prosperous country. "The North would have developed a strong industrial economy," says Bolton, "but it would have been more like France than the United States as we know it today. It wouldn't have been the big dog on the world stage."

Could it Happen?

The Civil War was a lot of things—an important fight for freedom, a tragic conflict between former countrymen and relatives—but the one thing it wasn't was a close call. Any chances the South had of winning disappeared early in the war, when the Confederacy might have received support from England or France. But the North always had more resources: more than double the population, a stronger economy, and more weapons. "Once [the] North geared up," says Bolton, "they had more people, more resources, and eventually better military leadership." When the Confederate States Army lost a decisive battle at Gettysburg, Pennsylvania, in June 1863, it was only a matter of time before the South ran out of manpower and firepower. The best outcome that the Confederacy could have hoped for was some kind of truce with the Union Army—one that would let the C.S.A. continue to function as an independent nation in which slavery was still legal. But even then, the cease-fire would only last so long. "It's hard to imagine there wouldn't have been another conflict if the North had lost," says Bolton. "The North would have more people and more industry. It would have wanted a rematch."

HISTORY SWITCHED

A shattered United States would cause a ripple effect throughout world history. Powered by its mighty economy, for instance, America's support for the Allied forces of World War II made a big difference in the outcome of the war, which saw the end of Germany's Nazi regime. A weakened United States after its loss in the Civil War may never have entered the war. "Without [America's] help," says Bolton, "Europe might have become a fascist continent [ruled by a dictator]." And if the United States never developed into a superpower, it wouldn't have entered into a space race with the former Soviet Union, which means humanity may have never set foot on the moon!

THE SPACE RACE
BLASTS OFF

Tasks

From the Past

What if you worked one of these jobs from history?

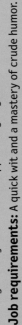

(3000 B.C. to the A.D. 1800s)

Court Jester

Throughout history, all the way back to ancient Egypt, people in power relied on live entertainment. (After all, Egyptian pharaohs and medieval kings could hardly surf the TV or the Internet.) The jester—part clown, part comedian—was the star of the court. He would crack jokes, juggle, dance, and even make fun of his powerful patrons, although some jesters were whipped for going too far.

Job requirements: A quick wit and a mastery of crude humor.

(Late 1600s to the early 1700s)

Caribbean Pirate

Captain Jack Sparrow from those Pirates of the Caribbean movies might seem like the sort of high-seas rogue you would invite to dinner, but real buccaneers would sooner clean out your house than clean their plates. These tough "freebooters" relied on their cutthroat reputation to frighten ships into surrendering. They also had it rough. Lousy food, cramped quarters, stinky crewmates, shipwrecking storms, and frequent sea battles were all part of the job in the "golden age of piracy." Still, a pirate's life was better than serving with the British or French navies. Unlike aboard navy vessels, pirate crews shared equally in the plunder and could vote in a new captain at any time should the current one fail to deliver.

Job requirements: Sailing skills, resistance to seasickness, and a bloodthirsty appetite for booty.

Noble Lord and Lady

(A.D. 1000 to 1500)

Empowered with a noble title from the various kings across Europe, this couple was in charge of their castle and the lands around it. It was the lord's job to protect these lands and administer the king's justice. The lady oversaw much of the household, including the kitchens and seamstresses who made clothing.

Job requirements: Lords and ladies were often born into the job. Noble boys inherited their titles and castles from their fathers, while noble girls were married off to other noble families to strengthen alliances.

Astronomer

Today, everyone knows that the sun—not the Earth—sits at the center of the solar system, and no one would call you crazy for saying the moon is pocked with craters or that the sun has spots. For an astronomer working in Europe before the 1600s, these ideas weren't just crazy—they were dangerous! The Roman Catholic Church decreed that all the planets, moons, and stars in the heavens were perfect spheres that orbited the Earth, which sat motionless at the center of all creation. Around the mid-1500s, scholars such as Nicolaus Copernicus and Galileo Galilei figured out that the Earth and its fellow planets actually orbit the sun. But stating these beliefs was dangerous in the time of the Roman Inquisition, when church officials tortured and even killed people who spoke against the church doctrine. When Galileo published a book that supported Copernicus's point of view, he was summoned to Rome and charged with heresy—the crime of teaching against the church's beliefs. He was put under house arrest and forbidden from publishing any more books. But Galileo defied the church's sentence and continued to experiment and write until his death.

Job requirements: Mathematical aptitude, an ability to use primitive telescopes and other instruments, and supreme courage to teach your observations despite threats from the church.

Cowboy

Saddle up, buckaroo. You might think cowboys only had a home where the buffalo roamed in the American West and routinely traded shots with quick-drawing gunslingers like Billy the Kid, but their history goes back further: to medieval Spain. Cowboys worked the range and tended cattle, keeping them safe from sickness, predators, and thieves (or cattle rustlers). "Cowboy" is still a valid career today, and you can sample life in the saddle at a dude ranch. (Don't feel left out, cowgirls—"dude" is slang for city slicker.)

Job requirements: Outdoor-survival skills, a good chili recipe, and your own horse.

History's Cruelest Careers...

LEECH COLLECTOR: Healers from the Middle Ages through the 19th century paid handsomely for leeches, but that didn't make the job of gathering these bloodsuckers any less ghastly. Collectors waded through worm-infested waters, using their bare legs as bait. Infection was a common on-the-job hazard.

SEARCHER OF THE DEAD: One out of every six Londoners perished from the bubonic plague in 1665. Searchers of the dead had the grim job of going door to door and carting away the corpses, risking infection from the Black Death at each stop.

GONG FARMER: Charged with cleaning the cesspits beneath castle garderobes—or bathrooms—and 16th-century homes in Europe, the gong farmer was a human pooper scooper. The job paid well, but hard-working farmers often found themselves up to their necks in doo-doo.

Chapter 5:
TECH CHECKED

Please turn off your smartphone. Lock away your game systems and music players. Disconnect all laptops, tablets, smartwatches, and i-toasters from the Internet. In fact, just unplug every gadget in your house. The next 18 pages are going to reboot the way you play with your most essential technology—and possibly give you a head start on tomorrow's state of the art. Don't worry: You'll get your gadgets back at the end of the chapter.

What Would Happen if...

What if the **Internet** was **never invented**?

Error 404— Web Pages Do Not Exist

You browse it over your breakfast cereal. Your parents use it to stream movies and music. Grandma and Grandpa send holiday cards over it. More than two billion people across the world rely on the Internet for instant information, communication, social-ization, and entertainment, making it one of the most important inventions in human history. But no single inventor can claim credit for this planet-spanning network, which dates back to more than 50 years ago, when computer scientists began brainstorming a system for researchers, educators, and government agencies to share information through their computers. The primitive network evolved over many upgrades into the modern Internet and the World Wide Web, the system of linked pages that most people browse online. It's become such a part of daily life that people panic when they can't connect. Now imag-ine if it never existed at all ...

Bye-bye, Wi-Fi

Forget Tweeting, updating your status, and sharing videos of your dog barreling through the screen door. If you want to let friends know what you're having for dinner in a world without the World Wide Web, you'll need to send a text, talk on the phone, or—gasp!—write a letter. Shopping for movies or music will involve a trip to the mall to buy "physical media": printed books, movies on Blu-ray Disc, and music on CD. No more Googling song lyrics on your smartphone or look-ing up the capital of North Dakota on Wikipedia. You'll need to go to the library or look it up in an encyclope-dia. Now you're researching like it's 1989!

Missing Links

A webless world wouldn't have to feel disconnected. Instead of broadband and Wi-Fi, we might see the rise of something like the Minitel service, a system of terminals launched in France and other countries in the 1980s. The network offered many of the modern Internet's features—the ability to make hotel reservations, check the weather, and shop—over telephone lines. "Something like that might have been developed in conjunction with something like the original Netflix [movie service], only for books and music, too," says historian Edward Tenner. A more low-tech look at a world without Internet comes from Cuba, an island nation lacking high-speed connectivity options. Cubans share entertainment and information through *El Paquete Semanal*—Spanish for "The Weekly Package"—an underground network of portable hard drives passed from person to person. Instead of logging online, *El Paquete*'s participants have created their own nationwide network made of people.

Side Effects Include ...

TROLL-FREE CALLING

The Internet, for all it has done to spread knowledge and shrink the world, has in some ways pushed people further apart. Humans evolved as social animals with brains wired for face-to-face interaction. Web browsers remove the faces from conversations while adding anonymity, letting complete strangers behave badly without consequences. The result: Armies of jerks lurk online, and even the most mundane topics set off these cyber-bullying "trolls." A world without the Internet would leave trolls with no place to hide.

MASSIVELY SINGLE-PLAYER GAMING

Without the web to link thousands of players into massively multiplayer worlds, gaming would revert to the good old days of split-screen play on a single television. In other words, opponents in *Mario Kart* would sit across the couch instead of across the country.

Could it Happen?

Not a chance. The Internet exists today because bigwigs in the U.S. government saw the value of a computer network that would operate even if bits of it were destroyed in a war. What started as a link between four computers has grown into a network of at least 75 million servers. Despite the occasional outage from your cable provider, the Internet is much too big to fail.

What if

you took a **time machine** back in time and **met yourself**?

It would be an encounter you'd either never forget or never remember ...

In an earlier *What Would Happen?* adventure, you took a spin through the dim past in your own time machine, all the way back to the origins of life on Earth. Now let's dust off that temporal transporter one more time for a quicker time trip: to last Thursday for a visit with a slightly younger you! Such an encounter raises all sorts of head-spinning questions. Wouldn't you remember meeting yourself before you left? Could you actually tweak the past to change the future? Is such a mind-blowing meeting even possible? The answers, it turns out, are maybe, maybe, and maybe! Astrophysicists—scientists who study the laws of physics that govern time and space—theorize that the outcome of any encounter with a younger you depends on the nature of our universe ... or universes. See for yourself as you visit *yourself* in this quick dash to the past ...

Hey, Yous!

Fffffzzzt ... pop! In a cloud of fizzy vapor and a flash of purple light, your time machine materializes right before the startled eyes of your younger self. "Hi, me," you say as you climb from the machine and stick out your hand. "I'm a slightly older you. What's new?" Your younger self returns the handshake while eyeing you warily, but neither of you melts into a puddle of goop or passes out from shock—typical reactions when this sort of thing happens in sci-fi movies. So far, so good! In fact, you haven't even broken any laws of physics.

But what happens next is up for scientific debate over the structure of our universe and its rules of cause and effect. Astrophysicists theorize that the universe we call home might actually be one of many, many, many alternate "parallel" universes in an endless "multiverse." "Instead of time lines wrapping themselves through a single universe," says astrophysicist Geraint F. Lewis, "they might loop through multiple universes." So when you warp back to last Thursday to visit your younger self, you're visiting a time and a place in a different universe from your own. The you you're meeting isn't actually you, and the past you're visiting isn't actually your past. This is an alternate universe, with alternate versions of you and your friends, and a future that diverges from your own.

That means you won't see any of the consequences of your visit when you return to your own timeline. Those changes will take place in the alternate universe's future. In fact, a multiverse has a different universe for every possible event and outcome. "Time travel is, at some level, weaving our way through them all," explains Lewis.

Side Effects Include ...

CHANGING TIMES

If you were hoping to share secrets of the future with your past self (such as the answers to Monday's pop quiz in history class) and then reap the benefits in your own timeline, you're out of luck—at least in a multiverse model of the universe. The alternate you will benefit from this information, but you won't have aced your history quiz in your own timeline. Better luck next timeline!

REMEMBER ME?

If you traveled back in time to meet your younger self, then you should remember meeting your older self right before you went back in time, right? But that's not the case in a multiverse. Remember: The younger you you're visiting isn't really you—it's an alternate you who will remember the encounter only in the alternate timeline. "You could remember meeting yourself," says Lewis, "but the you doing the remembering might be in a different future (universe) to the one you came from."

TIME OUT

So far we've considered time travel only in a multiverse with infinite alternate timelines. But what if this model doesn't reflect reality? Perhaps we live in a single universe with just one timeline? In this case, changing the past to alter the future wouldn't be an option. "Everything is locked in," says Lewis. "The future will be as written as the past. You would remember meeting yourself, and you will be compelled to travel through time to meet yourself."

TIME TRAVEL: A MATTER OF WHEN AND WHERE

A WRINKLE IN TIME AND SPACE

Could it Happen?

Although no one has invented a time machine (yet), some scientists do believe that travel back in time is possible. According to one theory, a time traveler would just need an intense source of gravity, the bigger the better, such as a black hole or even a pair of them orbiting each other at speeds approaching the velocity of light. Such an intense gravitational field would warp the fabric of space and time, folding and twisting it back on itself so the past and present actually touch in different times and places. Of course, you'd also need a time machine that could harness such planet-smashing forces and process some seriously complex physics equations to navigate this.

"Nothing in physics prevents time travel."
—Astrophysicist Geraint F. Lewis

What if cars drove themselves?

Computers in control means safe roads and plenty of leg room!

As far as animals that can operate automobiles go (a less exclusive group than you might think, including a dog named Porter and Cappy the chimpanzee), humans are best suited to sit behind the wheel. But that doesn't mean we're perfect. Lead-footed drivers speed up to race yellow lights. Rubber-neckers slow down to inspect fender benders on the side of the road, which leads to more accidents and backs up traffic. Internet-addicted drivers fiddle with their phones while cruising down the highway. Robot driving systems don't have these dangerous habits, which is why self-driving cars are such a smart idea. But would becoming a permanent passenger take the pleasure out of Sunday drives or make getting to your destination more than half the fun? Buckle up as we take a spin in a world of automated automobiles ...

Easy Riding

Human drivers must rely on their limited senses—sight, sound, and the feel of the road through the steering wheel. Robo-chauffeurs have access to a range of more powerful sensors. Using cameras, radar, and lasers, automatic-driving systems perceive a 360-degree view of the road. They can track multiple passing cars that would otherwise fall into a human driver's "blind spots" between the vehicle's side mirrors, dashboard, and chassis. The car's computer can access traffic data online and combine that information with a GPS system to plot the shortest routes to destinations. They can even communicate with each other using rapid bursts of data to warn of lane changes or sudden stops. And unlike human drivers, robots give their undivided attention to the task at hand: getting you to your destination safely.

All these high-tech features add up to cars that would drive faster, offer a smoother ride, get you to where you're going sooner, and make the roads safer. Gone will be the speed demons, sluggish Sunday drivers, sleepy truck drivers, and behind-the-wheel texters. Human error will still present a threat as long as drivers can take the wheel. But as you'll see in the next section, the days of you driving yourself may be numbered.

Driver's Ed: Auto-Auto Milestones

SELF-DRIVING CAR

1984: The Navlab at Carnegie Mellon University in Pennsylvania, U.S.A., begins experimenting with cars, vans, SUVs, and buses that can drive themselves using sensors to detect obstacles.

2012: Web giant Google begins developing autonomous cars that use lasers to scan the road and maintain a safe distance from other vehicles. Except for one minor fender bender with a bus, the program has had a clean accident record—at least when the cars aren't in "manual mode" (aka under human control).

TESLA CAR EQUIPPED WITH AUTOPILOT

2016: Electric-car manufacturer Tesla unveils an "Autopilot" feature for owners of its expensive Model S car. Although not a full-featured self-driving mode, Autopilot automatically changes lanes if the driver engages the turn signal, hunts for parking (and parks by itself), and steers the car in its current lane—although drivers are encouraged to keep their hands on the wheel at all times. Autopilot has already been credited with avoiding one accident.

Could it Happen???

A ROOMY ROBOCAR FROM MERCEDES-BENZ

Self-driving cars have been in development for decades, and several models are on the road now. Some offer basic features that assist the driver with tasks such as parallel parking and emergency braking. More expensive cars handle all the driving duties while allowing the human driver to take over at any time. These so-called autonomous cars still have steering wheels and other controls similar to standard cars, and people can still drive the old-fashioned way if they want to. True self-driving cars, set for the near future, won't have any controls at all. Travelers will use their smartphones to summon one of these auto-taxis from a fleet of robotic cars. Because these smart cars lack steering wheels and pedals, all passengers (yes, even Porter the pooch and Cappy the chimp) will have more room to stretch out and enjoy the ride.

Ready for Liftoff

What if we had flying cars?

Zipping to the mall in a sleek jet-powered sedan might seem like the coolest way to travel—at least according to sci-fi movies that predicted we'd all be soaring through the sky in the family car by now—but there's a reason we're still stuck on the ground in highway traffic. While self-driving cars might keep passengers safer, flying cars could spell disaster. When cars break down, drivers can simply pull over to the side of the road. Pilots in malfunctioning flying cars have nowhere to go but down. And even if flying-car designers eliminated the risk of pilot error by building only computer-controlled drones, mechanical errors could still result in deadly crashes.

That hasn't stopped inventors from developing many flying car proto-types—such as the sporty Moller Skycar—over the decades, but these flying machines are still too tricky for the average driver to operate without a pilot's license. They also often involve time-consuming trans-formations—wings that fold, propellers that tuck away, etc.—to get air-borne, making them more like planes that can drive on the road rather than true flying cars. Flying cars are also too slow and lack the passenger capacity to replace travel passenger airlines. For the foreseeable future, at least, cross-country trips will start with a drive to the airport.

Flight of Fancy: the Mizar Skycar

In the early 1970s, an American inventor named Henry Smo-linski bolted the wings and engine of a small airplane to the body of a compact Ford automobile. Named the Mizar, his prototype had the potential—and the risks—associated with all flying cars. Pilots could drive their Mizar-compatible car to the airport, install its wings, fly to a faraway airstrip, remove the wings, and cruise away. But Smolinski's prototype crashed and burned. A 1973 test flight ended in disas-ter when the strut holding the Mizar's right wing broke soon after takeoff. The wing snapped off and the Mizar crashed. It never flew again.

THE MIZAR AIRCRAFT MERGED CAR AND PLANE.

What if you had a hoverboard?

They glide over the ground without making a sound and cruise over terrain—from weedy fields to mucky ponds—where the most daring skateboarders fear to tread. Hoverboards (or skateboards that levitate on a cushion of gravity-defying energy) are the must-have toy of 2015, at least according to the Back to the Future time-travel films. But 2015 came and went, and the only "hoverboards" you'll find in stores today still rely on one of humanity's oldest inventions: the wheel.

A real-life hoverboard would offer the ultimate one-person thrill ride. Because it skims above the ground rather than on it, the board would go much farther on a single kick and provide a ride free of bumps and lurching stops. It could also do triple duty as a snowboard and water ski, making it three boards for the price of, well, probably 10 (a real-life hoverboard would be a toy for the wealthy).

Meanwhile, the technology powering the board's levitation abilities would show up in surprising places. Big vehicles and big cities are a bad combination, leading to a revolution in one-person "personal transportation vehicles" such as the Segway scooter. A hoverboard would become the hottest product in this market, which means you might share a "personal-transportation lane" with a hip executive scooting home from the office on a hoverboard modified with handlebars.

A PROTOTYPE HOVERBOARD TAKES FLIGHT.

Close Enough: Two True Hoverboards

Antigravity fields exist only in science fiction, but that hasn't stopped engineers from figuring out other ways to make boards hover. For instance ...

Hendo hoverboard
What makes it hover? Magnetism.
The good news is this skateboard-size contraption levitates above the ground just like a sci-fi hover-board. The bad news is the hovering effect only works over a special metallic surface, which creates a slight repelling force when it interacts with electromagnets built into the board's bottom.

ArcaBoard
What makes it hover? Fan propulsion.
The $15,000 ArcaBoard looks more like a giant flying domino than a hoverboard, but its bulky size is necessary to accommodate the 36 high-powered fans that propel the board and its rider up to a foot (30 cm) above land or sea.

THE ARCABOARD RIDES ON A CUSHION OF AIR.

What if

Now we see you. Now we don't!

Look at you, just sitting there letting all that light bounce off your head, shoulders, knees, and tennis shoes. You know everyone can see you, right? Of course you do! (Nice kicks, by the way.) That's literally how vision works: Light travels from the sun (or some other light source like a lightbulb or campfire) and reflects off objects in the environment into our eyes, which focus the light into visual information that our brains can understand. Curves and angles scatter light in a different way, which our brain perceives as ... well, curves and angles. What if you could short-circuit the entire process—and disappear from view—by slipping on some sort of invisibility cloak? Hey, why should kid wizards have all the fun?

Out of Sight

Elaborate magic tricks, sneaky spy missions, the world's best surprise parties—the list of fun functions for a real-life invisibility cloak is endless. But uses for such spiffy technology go way beyond pranks and hocus-pocus. Such a miracle fabric could actually save energy—and lives. House walls and roofs, for instance, could be switched into transparent mode to let in natural light and help heat the house with sunlight on cool, sunny days. Airline pilots and automobile drivers could make the chassis of their planes and cars see-through to eliminate blind spots or avoid backing into people. Surgeons could drape a fabric over their arms to see through their hands as they operate on patients.

And invisibility is just the beginning. The materials used to create these cloaks—exotic "metamaterials" (more on those in a bit)—have a wide range of uses beyond just fooling the human eye. They can manipulate sound and heat as well as light, meaning these materials could be used in everything from deep space for communication systems to the human body to zap tumors and even in ultrafast computers. So while an invisibility cloak would certainly liven up any party, the technology behind it would improve your quality of life.

Side Effects Include ...

SNEAK ATTACKS

Armies, navies, and air forces around the world have already invested billions in stealth technology that allows their soldiers and vehicles to remain unseen and unheard—at least to radar detection and heat sensors. True invisibility from sight as well as sensors is the next frontier of sneaky combat. Militaries around the world would have already begun an arms race to develop the next best cloaking devices—and the technology to see through them.

SIGHT GAGS

Any material capable of hiding a person or object would also be able to disguise it. Invisibility cloaks could transform eyesore cell phone towers into majestic redwood trees or turn construction sites into 3-D previews of the buildings to come. A scientist working on a cloaking fabric in Berkeley, California, U.S.A., envisions cloaking bandages that hide pimples and shirts that disguise belly flab as six-pack abs!

A SNEAKY OCTOPUS

The ability to cloak and hide in plain sight already exists in the wild. Color- and texture-shifting cells in the skin of octopuses, squids, and cuttlefish, for instance, allow them to blend seamlessly with rocks and morph into corals. Researchers studying these marine masters of disguise have begun to understand their tricks. Already scientists in California have developed a type of color-shifting "squid tape" that soldiers can wrap around their uniforms to add another layer of camouflage. In fact, all the cloaking concepts described on these pages—from see-through surgeon's hands to transparent cockpits—are real prototypes based on a variety of "active camouflage" technologies.

The simplest prototypes use cameras and displays to project the background onto an object, giving the illusion that it's transparent. More complex cloaking systems rely on lenses to bend light around objects, rendering them invisible if you look from precisely the right angle. The most advanced invisibility cloak is made of metamaterials that—like a charmed object from the world of Harry Potter—defy the laws of nature. Instead of reflecting or scattering light like normal fabrics, these materials make it appear as if light is passing through flat and curved surfaces. Someday they might be woven into a real-life invisibility cloak. Today, they can only be manufactured on a small scale, not even large enough to cloak a grain of sand.

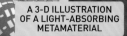

A 3-D ILLUSTRATION OF A LIGHT-ABSORBING METAMATERIAL

What if

They wouldn't threaten our lives, but they might threaten our jobs.

That robot vacuum slurping dust bunnies beneath your bed might seem pretty clever when it dodges table legs and your kitty's tail. And those millions of robots building everything from cars to candy bars in factories across the world work with a speed and precision that is well beyond human limits. But none of these machines—not even the mightiest supercomputers running the most advanced programs—can process the deep thoughts of that wrinkly three-pound (1.4-kg) melon of nerve cells between your ears. Your brain empowers you to laugh, cry, dream, paint, juggle a soccer ball, and learn. It's been called the most complex object in the universe, and computer scientists have been studying how to replicate its abilities in silicon for decades. What if they succeeded in making a machine as smart as you—or smarter?

STUDENT BUILDING A ROBOT

Trained Brain

Ever since the term "artificial intelligence" (A.I.) was coined in 1956 to describe the new field of building intelligent machines, computer scientists have devised robots and computers that mimic our abilities, from beating champions at chess to translating foreign languages as they're spoken. But one concept that remains beyond the reach of silicon-based smarts is self-awareness. "It's a key part of human-level intelligence," says roboticist Hod Lipson, director of the Creative Machines Lab at Cornell University in New York, U.S.A. "Self-awareness is the ability to 'simulate' oneself into the future, to learn and adapt, and plan using imagined experiences."

Being self-aware isn't just the ability to think—it's the ability to think about thinking. It's not the sort of command or concept that can be coded into a computer from the "top down," as computer scientists call programming specific functions into a machine. Instead, the machine must be designed from the "bottom up" to simulate a human brain: a network of 100 billion neuron nerve cells (also known as a neural network) that processes and stores information. Once this silicon brain is built and switched on, it will look after its own education—what computer scientists call machine learning. "You don't program machine learning," says Lipson. "You give it experiences and hope that it learns correctly. It's no different than teaching a child. You can't program a child. You just shape their experiences and hope they learn the right things."

Two Dangers of Intelligent Machines
(that don't involve them wiping out the human race)

Creative Crash

If we let intelligent machines take over every human activity, then suddenly we're the ones in danger of becoming obsolete. "Once robots can do almost everything better than almost anyone," Lipson says, "people will lose the meaning they derive from the accomplishment of hard tasks. When that happens, a lot of social structure will begin to unravel."

A ROBO-WAITER SERVES MEALS TO CUSTOMERS AT A ROBOT-THEMED RESTAURANT.

Robots for the Rich

As machines take jobs away from people in every field—from medicine to entertainment—more and more people will find themselves unable to make a living. "The loss of jobs will increase the gulf between the haves and the have-nots," says Lipson. "Whoever owns the robots and the A.I. will own the wealth." Hopefully, artificial intelligence will be smart enough to solve any problems it creates.

> **Even human-centered tasks like teaching, taking care of children and the elderly will eventually be relegated to robots.**
> –Roboticist Hod Lipson

THIS ROBOTIC RECEPTIONIST WORKS AT A JAPANESE DEPARTMENT STORE.

See next page for more!

Give and Take

It's a story as old as Dr. Frankenstein's monster: Scientists create intelligent life, and then intelligent life turns on the scientists. In reality, a machine capable of human-level thought is more likely to save humanity than harm it. Such an artificial intelligence would combine a human's ability to learn with a computer's superhuman processing speed and perfect memory recall—without the need to snooze, take a bathroom break, or spend two weeks at a tropical resort to avoid burning out. Installed in a medical laboratory, an artificial intelligence could analyze the case histories of all cancers or some other disease to find a cure. Intelligent machines could study and offer solutions to humanity's greatest threats, from climate change to species extinctions. Installed on a spaceship, an A.I. would serve as our eyes and ears—and brains—as it unravels the mysteries of the solar system.

Robots began replacing human workers in factories decades ago, but an intelligent, self-aware machine is capable of much more than doing our dirty jobs. "Intelligent robots will gradually take over every human endeavor," says Lipson. "Not just medical and legal work, but also creative endeavors, like design, art, and scientific discovery." The sequel to *Frankenstein* might be written, directed, and rendered by the A.I. itself.

A.I. Breakthroughs: Giant Leaps for Robotkind

Shakey Sets a Course (1966):

Long before the Curiosity rover figured out how to navigate the surface of Mars without remote control from Earth and robot vacuums began bouncing off the walls of everyone's house, this wheeled contraption became the first robot to plot its own course through random environments. It used its built-in camera to map its surroundings, then rolled slowly, *slowly* from one side of the room to the other, avoiding obstacles.

ADVANCED PROGRAMS CAN DEFEAT HUMAN CHESS MASTERS.

Deep Blue Scores a Checkmate (1997):

Designed by IBM, the supercomputer Deep Blue accomplished what many thought was impossible: It defeated world chess champion Garry Kasparov—and it defeated him so soundly that Kasparov was convinced the computer had human help. Deep Blue's achievement is an example of top-down programming. It was coded specifically to play chess through pure computational brute force by calculating thousands of moves ahead. If you challenged it to checkers, however, Deep Blue wouldn't have a clue what to do.

$0

KEN

Could it Happen?

Computers in the 1950s were the size of a house—literally. Today, your vastly more powerful smartphone fits in the pocket of your jeans. Some computer scientists point to this explosive growth in computer might and miniaturization and predict we'll have self-aware, human-smart machines by 2050—or sooner. But not everyone is as optimistic. "Software does not improve as smoothly as hardware," says Lipson. To get a better idea of the timeline for self-aware A.I., he thinks we should look at how intelligence evolved in nature over millions of years rather than how

computers grew in power over the past few decades. It took Mother Nature 500 million years to achieve human-level intelligence after early life-forms began to develop eyesight, which itself took about 50 million years to develop in land-based life-forms. By comparison, Lipson explains, it took about 50 years for machines to develop reliable eyesight after the birth of the first robots. "Drawing on this analogy," Lipson predicts, "I believe that human-level, self-aware A.I. will be achieved around the year 2500."

Watson Wins (2011):

IBM followed up Deep Blue's success with a supercomputer designed to beat two former champions at a much more complicated game: the TV quiz show *Jeopardy!* Programmers used a bottom-up approach to teach the machine—named Watson—to understand spoken questions and retrieve the answers using thousands of processing cores and dozens of servers in a system similar to a human's neural network. Watson walloped his opponents. Today the computer helps doctors diagnose and treat patients.

$1,200

WATSON

JEOPARDY! CHAMPION KEN JENNINGS AND IBM COMPUTER WATSON

DeepMind Plays for Keeps (2016):

Artificial intelligence doesn't necessarily take the form of faceless monolithic mainframes or humanoid robots with high-def screens displaying cheery emoticons. The British A.I. company DeepMind, which was bought by Web giant Google in 2014, specializes in programs—called algorithms—that help neural networks learn to recognize speech or faces, or even how to beat video games. DeepMind's latest triumph, called AlphaGo, beat a champion of the strategy game Go, which is considered more complicated than chess.

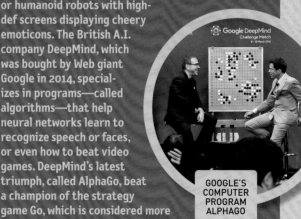

GOOGLE'S COMPUTER PROGRAM ALPHAGO

What if

No need to fuss if you miss the bus. "Beam" to class in a blink!

It's everyday technology in sci-fi books and Star Trek movies: Travelers step into a special teleportation chamber and—zap!—their bodies "dematerialize" into a glittering stream of atoms, which is then transmitted to a faraway destination. Here the atom stream "rematerializes" into the travelers, who step off the teleporter pad and go about their business. Teleportation technology would be both terrifying (you'd get blasted to your tiniest bits with each trip!) and terrific (no more frazzled nerves at crowded airports!). It would also change the world. Prepare to beam up as we turn science fiction into fact ...

Going Somewhere Fast

Imagine zipping to Switzerland for a chocolate bar, zapping to Southern California for a surf session, then materializing in math class moments before the school bell rings. A teleporter would certainly make the world feel smaller. Crossing the globe would take no more effort than a quick trip to your local teleportation station. Voyages in "old-fashioned" forms of transportation—planes, trains, automobiles, and cruise ships—would become an old-fashioned novelty for travelers with time to kill.

But instant transportation would revolutionize much more than the travel industry. Shipping companies could "upload" cars, building materials, mail—anything—into a sort of Internet of objects that could then be "downloaded" at their destinations. Surgeons could aim a teleportation beam at deadly tumors and beam them from the patient's body without the need for surgery and potential infections. Oil spills and other toxic wastes could get zapped directly into the sun, where they would melt harmlessly into vapor. Teleportation technology might help save the world as well as change it.

High Beam

No industry would benefit more from teleportation than the space program. Travel into space requires rockets that burn massive amounts of fuel to escape Earth's gravitational field just to carry a few astronauts and equipment into Earth's orbit, where gravity still holds sway. Teleportation technology would skip past gravity's grip, beaming explorers and parts for spaceships directly into Earth's orbit or beyond. Soon, every planet in the solar system would be linked with a teleportation station built from materials beamed from mining operations in the asteroid belt, which would serve as a shipyard for starships bound for distant stars. Just as teleportation originated in the realm of science fiction, it would help real-life astronauts explore where no one has gone before.

Side Effects Include ...

MOVING TARGETS

Sci-fi movies make teleporting from points A to B look as easy as 1, 2, 3, but a real-life teleportation system would need to calculate many factors to guarantee the traveler's safe arrival. The Earth is constantly in motion as it spins on its axis and orbits the sun (which is also moving around the galactic core). And different points on Earth move at different speeds depending on their distance from the Equator. If a teleporter didn't compensate for all this motion, travelers might arrive at their destination hurtling hundreds of miles an hour (ouch!), landing sideways or upside down on the other side of the world (awkward!), or materializing inside a solid wall (yikes!).

LOSING YOURSELF

Teleportation technology is more than just a puzzle for physicists and engineers. It also raises troubling philosophical questions. Each time a traveler teleports, after all, he or she is literally blasted to bits, neither dead nor alive until the machine reassembles his or her atoms at the destination point. Such technology could transport your body—tissue, blood, bones, and (hopefully) your clothes—but what about less physical characteristics such as your consciousness? Would everything that makes you *you* survive the transmission, or would the traveler who steps off the destination exist as a sort of clone who only thinks he or she is you? Your brain and its contents are so complex that, according to a team of German students, it would take trillions of years to transmit its structure and data using today's fastest radio technology.

Could it Happen?

Believe it or not, teleporting technology already exists, but it's not quite the crew-beaming transporter from *Star Trek*. Using a process called quantum teleportation, scientists have figured out how to transfer the characteristics of one atom (the basic unit of matter) to a distant atom. This is teleportation on the very smallest scale, but it's a start! Meanwhile, German scientists are teleporting objects by breaking them down and scanning them layer by layer, then re-creating them with a 3D printer (a machine that creates physical objects) at the destination point. Such technologies might eventually be used to transmit objects across the solar system. Teleporting people, however, is a trickier matter. The objects being "teleported" in both the examples above are destroyed at their point of origin and duplicated at their destination. Crowded airports don't sound so bad after all!

What if

you were bionic?

Web Head

Cybernetic implants will soon let us surf the Internet and make calls ... with our minds! "Already implants are placed deep in the brain of individuals in order to overcome the effects of Parkinson's disease, epilepsy, and depression," says Kevin Warwick, a cybernetics researcher at Coventry University in England. "In the near future many more neurological problems will be treated this way. But implants will also enable all of us to communicate just by thinking to each other when our brains are linked in to a matrix-like network."

Smart Skin

Forget your smartphone? Don't feel dumb! Special "dermal displays" implanted under your skin will let you watch movies, check "me-mails," and create animated temporary tattoos anywhere on your body.

Super Vision

Doctors use lasers to correct imperfections in patients' peepers today. Tomorrow they'll implant high-tech contact lenses and even cybernetic enhancements that'll let humans see farther, in the dark—even in psychedelic heat vision.

Could it Happen?

For the most part, it already has! All the bionic technology on these pages either exists now or will in the near future. To demonstrate how close technology has come to duplicating or enhancing the human body, a team of Swiss engineers collected the most state-of-the-art bionic parts—robotic arms, exosuit legs, artificial organs, and even a computerized brain—to create a walking, talking, breathing bionic man. Named Frank (after Frankenstein's monster), this cool-but-creepy robot replicates half of the human body, including a beating heart.

A PATIENT WITH THE PROTO1 BIONIC ARM

Spare Parts

Artificial limbs have been a huge help for people missing arms and legs because of birth defects, accidents, or combat injuries. Modern robotic limbs bend and grab just like the real thing while responding to input from the wearer's muscles. Scientists have already developed an artificial arm that plugs directly into the wearer's brain. The connection bypasses the spinal cord, giving paralyzed victims of spinal injuries the opportunity to walk and use their arms again.

Gut Check

A sickly spleen, bum lung, or even bad ticker will no longer lead to a deadly diagnosis. Scientists have developed artificial prototypes of all of these organs. Some of them have saved lives! Meanwhile, microscopic robots will replace your body's old cells and cure diseases, increasing your life span by hundreds of years, while "nutribot" pills will zap all the junk in your junk food, letting you binge on fatty burgers and candy bars without getting fat.

Brainy Brawn

Although bionic arms and legs can replace lost limbs, they're not strong enough to help with heavy lifting. For that you'll need to turn to "wearable robotics," mechanical outfits that grant incredible strength and endurance. "Strapping into one of these 'exosuits' will increase your muscle strength by a factor of 16 and allow you to manipulate heavy objects," says Jacob Rosen, director of the bionics lab at the University of California.

EXOSUIT

107

Chapter 6:
Natural Wonders

Take a second to step out the front door, suck in some fresh air, and wiggle your toes in the grass. You'll want one last moment to admire your one-of-a-kind world, because after this chapter it will never seem the same again. You're about to explore alternate Earths where the moon never rises, the oceans drain away, and the molten core of the planet gets a little too close for comfort. Earthlings, prepare for unearthly things ...

What if the sun suddenly disappeared?

What Would Happen if...

What if
the Earth was flat?

Falling off the world's edge wouldn't be a problem. Reaching the edge would be.

It's a popular myth that sailors in the 15th century believed the Earth was flat until Christopher Columbus sailed his fleet over the horizon and didn't plummet into space. But people have known the Earth was round for more than 2,000 years. A Greek mathematician named Eratosthenes even managed to calculate the distance around the planet some 1,700 years before Columbus was born! But not everyone is sold on the idea of a spherical world. Even today, despite globe-trotting air travelers and photographic evidence of a nearly round—or "oblate spheroid"—Earth seen from space, thousands of diehard science deniers insist our planet is shaped more like a pancake than a basketball. What if these members of the Flat Earth Society were actually right?

Funky in the Middle
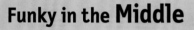

According to flat-planet proponents, Earth's landmasses and seas are all squished onto the surface of an enormous disc bordered at its rim by the icy wilderness of Antarctica. But if such a world actually existed under the normal laws of physics, its surface would seem like some oddball virtual-reality gamescape. Seas and lakes would puddle to the center of the disc, pooling like an ocean-size raindrop. The atmosphere, meanwhile, would compress into a bubble around this mega-puddle. Gravity on a disc-like world, it turns out, behaves much differently from what we're used to.

On a normal, nearly round world such as Earth, the trillions of tons of rock and molten metals beneath your toes generate an intense gravitational field that pulls everything—seas, continents, and the atmosphere above them—toward the planet's

MAP OF THE WORLD DRAWN IN 1511

core. A disc-like planet, however, is most dense at its middle and less so toward its rim. That makes gravity strongest at the center of the disc. So while a flat Earth might look like a plate, its gravitational field would work like a giant bowl, tugging everything toward the center. You would need a boat to stand near the middle of the disc—say, in Canada, which would sit leagues beneath the puddled ocean—but the views would be spectacular. From this high above the flat Earth's surface, on a clear day, you could see literally to the edge of the world.

PTOLEMY WORLD MAP CA A.D. 150

Side Effects Include ...

UPHILL AND AWAY

Traveling outward from the center of this disc-like world would feel like climbing a hill that becomes steadily steeper as you near the rim. By the time you hoof it to Antarctica at the world's edge, you'll need the skills and gear of a mountain climber to keep from tumbling toward your point of origin. Oh, and you better pack a space suit. By this point in your disc-world hike, you'll have trekked outside the limits of Earth's atmosphere.

LIVING ON THE EDGE

No need to worry about tumbling off the tip of the Earth once you clamber all the way to its rim. In fact, you'll actually need to pull yourself up onto the edge, just like you were summiting the face of a cliff. With the entirety of the planet's gravity pulling you toward the disc's center, the world's edge would become a perfectly safe place for a stroll. You could drop even a basketball over the edge, toward the center of the disc, and watch it roll all the way home.

NO SMOOTH SAILING AT THE EDGE OF A FLAT EARTH

Could it Happen?

Members of the Flat Earth Society have concocted all sorts of silly theories to explain a world that isn't round. The sun and moon, they say, are actually artificial light sources whirling through the sky to create the illusion of a spherical, spinning planet. NASA's space missions were all faked on elaborate movie sets. But you don't need to be a Greek mathematician to prove them wrong. Ships traveling over the horizon, for instance, disappear from the hull up as the curvature of the Earth obstructs your view from shore. During lunar eclipses, the Earth's shadow on the moon is obviously round. Then there's the straightforward fact that a flat Earth doesn't square with the laws of physics. "Such a world would be fundamentally unstable," says Neil Comins, a physics professor at the University of Maine. "It would have so much mass—meaning that it would have so much gravity—that as soon as it became flat for whatever reason, it would pull itself into an oblate spheroid like the Earth."

Alternate Worlds

What if the Earth was twice its size?

Brushing your teeth would be an upper-body workout. Walking to class would feel like running a marathon ... uphill! Why? Gravity, that force of attraction generated by every object in the universe (yes, including you), would suddenly get a big boost in intensity. Gravity is imperceptible on a small scale, but the larger an object is and the more matter it contains (its mass), the greater its gravitational tug. The Earth is a very big thing—composed of densely packed rocks and molten metals—so its gravity makes everything around it "fall" toward the planet's center.

If the Earth's diameter was suddenly doubled to about 16,000 miles (26,000 km)—becoming a "super-Earth," as astronomers call large Earthlike planets—gravity would double along with it (assuming its density remained the same). And the consequences would extend beyond the constant exhaustion of lugging around a second you. Famous landmarks—from Italy's Leaning Tower of Pisa to the Statue of Liberty's torch—would likely tumble. Tall trees—including the world's tallest, the redwoods—would uproot and topple with a thunderous crash.

In the long term, all Earthlings would need to evolve for life in a world where everything is twice as heavy. Humans and animals would become squat and stumpy. Trees would grow short and stumpy. Even the sky would take on a new look. The sudden doubling in the Earth's gravitational field would pull the moon apart. Its debris would form a ring around our world (which you'll get to see later in this chapter).

A Real Monster!

Astrophysicists once believed it was impossible for giant Earthlike planets to form (their intense gravity attracted gas, ballooning them into gas giants similar to Jupiter or Neptune). But then, in 2014, astronomers found a real monster-size planet. Named Kepler-10c after the star it orbits 560 light-years away in the constellation Draco, this rocky world is more than twice the size of ours and 17 times as dense, meaning its gravity is actually three times stronger. Don't expect any super-Earthlings, though. Astronomers believe Kepler-10c's surface is much too hot to support life.

What if the Earth was half its size?

With gravity suddenly cut in half, every jump shot would be a slam dunk. A snowboarding jaunt through the terrain park would launch you into the trees. You would feel like a huge weight has been lifted off your shoulders. But all's not well in a world where every kid could bench-press a motorcycle.

For a glimpse of life—or the lack of it—on a pipsqueak Earth, just look at Mars. Our planetary neighbor is half the size of Earth but less dense, meaning it weighs less and generates less gravity. If you weighed 100 pounds (45 kg) on Earth, you'd weigh 38 pounds (17 kg) on Mars. Anyone raised on the red planet would stand taller in the slighter gravity but would develop weaker bones and muscles. A trip back to Earth would be lethal. But the weaker gravity here has another consequence: Mars lost most of its atmosphere billions of years ago, when asteroid impacts blasted it into space. The air there today (mostly carbon dioxide) is too wispy to breathe or hold much heat—characteristics that are crucial for life as we know it. Scoring slam dunks might not be quite as fun if you have to wear a bulky space suit on the basketball court to do it.

The Lighter Side

Believe it or not, gravity's pull isn't the same—and your weight isn't 100 percent consistent—across the entire surface of the Earth. Remember, gravity is the force of attraction created by all matter, including all the rocks, dirt, minerals, and metals beneath your feet. But Earth's mass isn't distributed evenly throughout the planet. Canada's Hudson Bay region, for instance, has a slight dent in its crust left by sheets of ice that melted 20,000 years ago. As a result, gravity is slightly weaker here—but you'd never notice any boosts to your jump shots. The "missing" gravity is much too small to notice without incredibly sensitive instruments.

What if

Buildings would topple! Windstorms would rage! Seas would slosh into your bedroom!

Our world has whirled round and round since the formation of our solar system roughly 4.6 billion years ago, when whirlpools of dust and gas spun faster and faster until they collapsed under their own gravity into planets. With no force to counter-act its spinning motion, Earth retained the rotation from its early days. It rotates on its axis once every day, spinning along its Equator at the speed of a fighter jet. What if our planet suddenly hit the brakes? Not even the sturdiest seat belt would save you from a lethal lurch and wind blasts that make a hurricane seem like an afternoon breeze.

Brake Time

Aside from seeing the sun, moon, stars, and other heavenly objects wheel across the sky, you don't notice the rotation of the planet beneath your feet. We're all caught up in the motion of its spin and held to the surface by its gravity, along with the atmo-sphere around us, the bicycles and cars on the road, and the birds in the sky. But if the Earth suddenly stopped, that same momentum would send every-thing flying and scour the surface with hurricane-force winds.

People who lived closer to the Equator—where Earth's spin is the fastest—would have the roughest ride. In an instant, they would go from traveling at 1,070 miles an hour (1,720 km/h) to a complete stop. Everything around them—skyscrapers, shopping malls, soil, trees, seas, and even the atmosphere— would hurtle in the direction of the planet's former

spin at nearly its same speed. Only the sturdy bed-rock deep beneath your feet would remain in place. Gravity would keep everything from flying into space, but the Earth would become a different place for anyone who lived far enough from the Equator (where the Earth's rotation is slower) to have a softer landing and winds below tornado-strength.

Side Effects Include ...

TIME OFF

The Earth's daily spin sets the length of our day and gives us a good idea when to head home for dinner. With the planet on pause, a day would now last a year, because it would take 365 days for the sun to return to its original place in the sky. Noon would last a month, along with dawn and dusk. Imagine a month-long sunset!

HOT TOPIC

Your day at the beach might last nearly six months, but you'd need to slather on super-duper sunscreen to survive the unrelenting sunlight before bundling up for six months of night. Crops would also wither unless they were grown farther to the north or south of the Equator. The region around the Equator would swamp with seawater as the planet lost its slight bulge—and its spherical shape—a side effect of Earth's spin.

SHIELDS DOWN

The Earth's spin interacts with the planet's iron core to create a magnetic field that shields us from solar radiation and all but the strongest storms of charged particles thrown out by the sun. Without this natural force field, we Earthlings would be at greater risk from skin cancers and other life-ruining radiation hazards.

Could it Happen?

Fear not: This nightmare scenario is a virtual impossibility. Only a cataclysmic collision with a rogue planet or massive asteroid could bring the spinning Earth to a standstill. If that happened, we'd have much bigger problems. (Instant incineration, for starters!) The gradual slowing of the planet's spin is another story. Earth's rotation is actually decreasing because of the moon's gravitation pull, although it will take millions of years for us to notice.

What if

Life would go on— but not as we know it.

Think Earth is the most important spot in the solar system? Think again. The sun is the real star of the show. The closest star to Earth, it sits at the center of our solar system and accounts for 99.8 percent of the solar system's total mass (more than a million Earths would fit inside the sun). Despite its jumbo size, the sun is really just a big ball of mostly hydrogen gas. A process called nuclear fusion converts hydrogen to helium deep in the sun's core, where temperatures hit a toasty 27 million degrees Fahrenheit (15 million degrees Celsius). Fusion produces energy that pro-vides most of the heat and light on Earth. It's essential to *most* forms of life here. Why the emphasis on *most*? Let's flip off the sun's switch and see ...

EARTH'S CITY LIGHTS

Lights **Out**

If the sun suddenly vanished, you wouldn't have a clue at first. The sky would still be blue. Sunbathers could still soak up rays on the beach. The sun would appear in the sky like always. On the Earth's night side (the side pointed away from the sun), the moon would still shine with the sun's reflected rays against a backdrop of stars and planets. "We would have about eight minutes of bliss before reality sets in," says astrobiologist Jacob Haqq-Misra. Then, poof! The planet would plunge into the darkest night in history.

The Big Chill

Those campfires would soon become a crucial source of heat as well as light. Without solar energy to warm it, Earth's atmosphere would lose heat into space. Within a week, temperatures across the globe would drop to below freezing. In a year, average temperatures would drop to minus 100°F (-73°C). But Earth's core generates its own heat, and eventually the temperature would stop dropping—at a deadly minus 400°F (-240°C). To stand any chance of survival, humans would need to move their cities deep underground and tap into the Earth's internal heat—or geothermal energy—which is already the hot thing in countries such as Iceland.

The oceans, meanwhile, would ice over, but life would continue deep under the frozen surface. In the late 1970s, scientists studying the seafloor discovered geysers belching a boiling mineral-rich stew into the crushing depths of the ocean. These "hydrothermal vents" didn't just look like they were from outer space—they were actually teeming with alien-like life. Here, in the constant darkness, bacteria convert chemicals into food in a process called chemosynthesis. Shrimp, crabs, and eyeless tube-worms survive by feeding on these bacteria, creating a food chain completely independent of the sun. If humans can't figure out a way to survive the endless night, these deep-sea creatures would become Earth's dominant life-forms.

GIANT TUBE WORMS

Why the eight-minute wait? Light travels really, really, *really* fast—as in 186,282 miles a second (299,792 km/s)—but the sun is also really, really far away (about 38,000 times the distance between New York City and Los Angeles). It takes eight minutes and 20 seconds for the light leaving the sun to reach Earth and your eyeballs. So, if the sun suddenly winked out of existence, it would take eight minutes and 20 seconds for the sun's final rays to reach us. Then, darkness. Anyone watching the moon would see it go black, like a nightlight switched off, as sunlight stopped reflecting off its surface. Mars would wink out within the next 10 minutes to an hour, depending on its distance from the Earth and the sun. The outer planets would gradually vanish over the next several hours as the last rays of sunlight left the solar system and stopped reflecting from its heavenly bodies. The only light on Earth would be starlight and artificial light—electric light, gaslight, and (when the fossil fuels ran out) campfires.

SOLAR ECLIPSE

See next page for more!

Side Effects of a Vanishing Sun Include ...

SPACESHIP EARTH

The sun's enormous gravity is the glue that holds the solar system together. If the sun suddenly vanished, the solar system would come unglued. Every planet would hurl into space along its current trajectory, like a rock released from a string whirled over your head. All the dwarf planets, asteroids, and comets, meanwhile, would eddy around each other or fall under the sway of the next largest heavenly body in the vicinity (most likely Jupiter, the second largest object in the solar system after the sun).

DELAYED REACTION

As strange as it might sound, gravity isn't an instantaneous force. Gravitational fields actually travel at the same speed as light, which means we Earthlings wouldn't notice we were free from the sun's gravity until eight minutes and 20 seconds after it vanished—or at the same moment the sun winked out as its final rays reached our eyes. Earth would suddenly become a rogue planet, hurtling through space for thousands or millions of years until it fell under the gravitational sway of a distant star or black hole.

HEAVENLY BODIES DRIFT WILLY-NILLY.

THE SUN WILL BURN OUT, BUT NOT FOR BILLIONS OF YEARS.

STALE AIR

While chemosynthesis would continue near hydrothermal vents deep under the ocean's now-frozen surface, the process of photosynthesis—during which plants and trees use sunlight to convert carbon dioxide from the air into energy-rich sugars and oxygen—on land will shut down immediately. The tallest trees might live for decades on sugars stored in their bark, but other plants would perish immediately and oxygen levels in the atmosphere would plummet.

A DEEP-SEA VENT SPEWS ITS CHEMICAL STEW.

BROKEN CHAIR

Hope you stocked up on canned chili before the sun bid goodbye. Animals that live off plants would be the next to go, followed by the animals that eat these animals. The food chain would fall apart from the bottom up, and humans would need to find a new food source—perhaps algae grown by artificial light, which would also help boost our oxygen levels—to survive this new age of perpetual darkness.

HALOPHYTE:
A PLANT THAT GROWS IN WATERS OF HIGH SALINITY

Could it Happen? ???

Breathe easy: The sudden disappearance of the sun is impossible. But here's the bad news (for your distant, distant relatives in the far future, at least): The sun's core will run out of hydrogen fuel eventually. When that happens, its core will heat up and expand outward—possibly reaching all the way to Earth in a vibrant cloud known as a red dwarf. It will appear as a beautiful nebula to distant star systems, but the view won't be so pretty from here. Fortunately, we won't start to see the effects of the sun's demise for at least a billion years.

What if

you **dug a hole** to the **other side** of the **Earth** ?

You'd get boiled, squashed, or drowned—unless you found a high-tech ride ...

You'd need more than a shovel and a strong back to hack a hole through the planet. Earth's insides are a dangerous place, fraught with dead ends for anyone foolish enough to dig deep without donning something more durable than a hard hat. You would need a superpowered drilling vehicle combining the indestructibility of Iron Man with the rock-smashing strength of the Incredible Hulk. Such a vehicle doesn't exist in the real world, but you're about to board one for the sake of this scenario. Ready? Strap yourself into the cockpit of the Drilldozer!

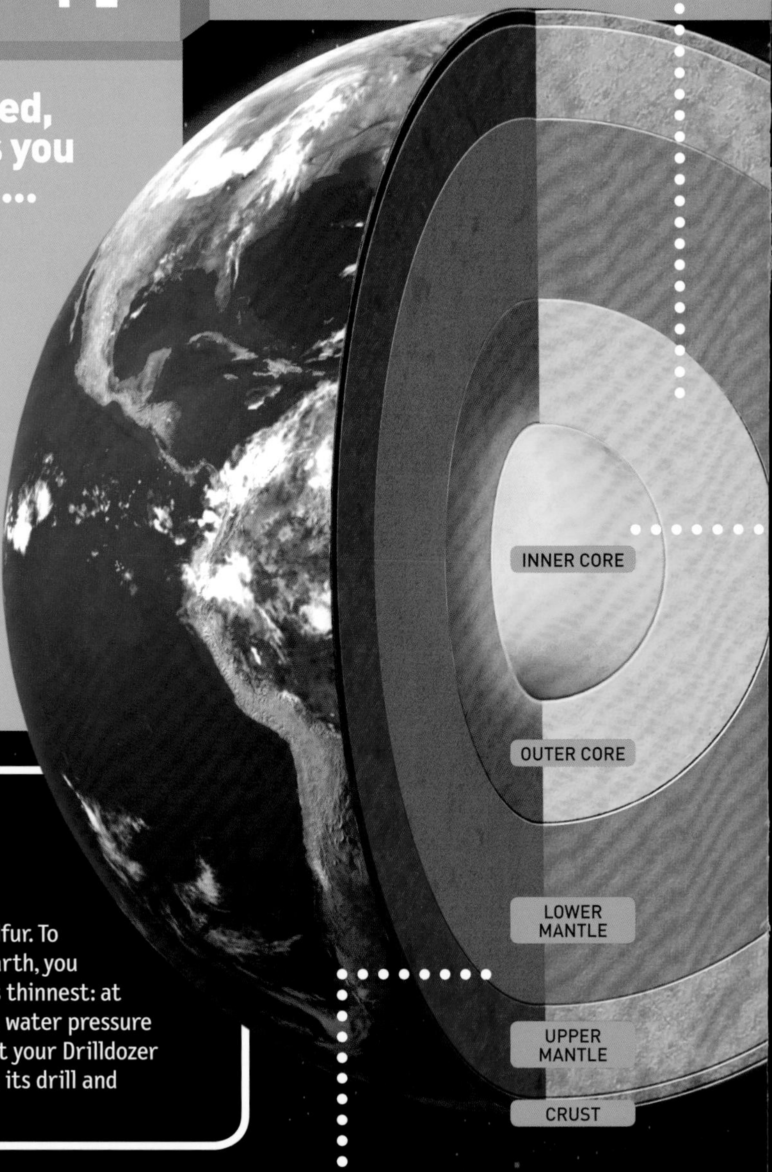

INNER CORE

OUTER CORE

LOWER MANTLE

UPPER MANTLE

CRUST

1

Going Down! Your first obstacle lies right beneath your feet: The planet's crust. Earth's outer layer is up to 47 miles (75 km) thick in places and laced with hazards, from pockets of molten rock to lakes of boiling sulfur. To shave some time off your trip through the Earth, you start your drilling mission where the crust is thinnest: at the bottom of the deepest ocean trench. The water pressure down here would crush a Navy submarine, but your Drilldozer is built to withstand far worse. Let's activate its drill and start digging!

2

Hot Pockets Don't bother celebrating once you've dug through the planet's crust. You've literally just scratched the surface of the planet. Below lies the mantle, a layer of semi-molten metals such as iron, magnesium, and aluminum. If you happen to uncover any minerals that look like pieces of glittering glass on your way down, scoop them up! The heat and pressure down here are intense enough to compress carbon into diamonds, the hardest natural material on Earth. Your Drilldozer's drill is tipped with diamond, so these minerals might come in handy as spares.

3 Core Breach Bust through the mantle and you encounter a spherical Mars-size sea of molten iron and nickel swirling 1,800 miles (2,900 km) beneath the surface. Welcome to the outer core. It flows around an inner core of iron two-thirds the size of the moon. Temperatures here exceed 10,000°F (5600°C)—hotter than the surface of the sun—yet the intense pressure here locks the molten iron into a solid sphere. Good thing the Drilldozer has air-conditioning!

4 Going Up! Aside from the crushing pressure it creates around you, gravity is your best buddy during the long haul to the center of the Earth. It's all downhill to the Earth's inner core, after all, and you actually experience zero gravity at the exact center of the planet. But you've only made it to the halfway point. It's time to begin the uphill battle to dig your exit tunnel through the opposite half of the planet. That's roughly 3,958 miles (6,370 km) of molten metal and solid rock you'll need to dig through, all of it bouncing off your Drilldozer's hull. Air pressure at the Earth's center will be 3.5 million times what you feel on the planet's surface. Your body would suffer serious damage once you hit 27 times the surface pressure! Please keep your arms and legs inside the Drilldozer at all times as you climb up, up, and up toward the planet's surface.

Side Effects Include ...

WET EXIT

More than 70 percent of the Earth's surface is covered with water, which means you're much more likely to strike seawater than sunlight when you finally reach the other side of the planet. If you tried to dig the proverbial hole to China from the United States, you'd end up all wet under the Indian Ocean. (If you really wanted to dig to China, you'd have to start your descent in Argentina instead.)

RAPID TRANSIT

World travelers will appreciate your shortcut through the soil. A plane trip across half the world takes at least a day by airplane. Going through the world instead of around it would get you there in a fraction of the time—as long as you sucked all the air from the tunnel and figured out a way to protect your passenger craft from the punishing force of the Earth's rotation.

Could it Happen?

Not a chance. The trip is just too treacherous! Despite using mid-ocean ridges as a head start for their digging operations, no one has been able to pierce even the Earth's crust. The deepest hole ever dug—the Kola Superdeep Borehole in northwest Russia—is just 7.6 miles (12 km) deep. That drilling operation ground to a halt in 1992 when the drill hit a pocket of extreme temperatures.

Earth Oddities

What if Earth wasn't tilted on its axis?

Our home planet is a slouch, tilted 23.5 degrees off of its axis of rotation. This imperfect posture is the reason we have four seasons. As it orbits the sun, the planet's tilt exposes more or less of the Northern and Southern Hemispheres to the sun depending on the time of year. When the South Pole is pointed toward the sun, Australia and other countries south of the Equator receive more direct sun exposure, resulting in warm summer temperatures. At the same time, the North Pole is tilted away from the sun, reducing sun exposure and making for chilly winter temperatures.

Without its tilt, Earth would be a much more boring planet. Instead of seasons, the weather would be much more uniform year-round, affected only by local storms and the gradual effects of climate change. Regions that see snowy winters and pleasant summers with the tilt would end up locked in a perpetual autumn. "Winter" and "summer" would be destinations rather than times of the year. You'd have to travel farther north or south of the Equator if you wanted to go skiing, while summer would exist solely in the tropics. Nearly every day of the year would have 12 hours of daylight and 12 hours of darkness, except at the poles, which would experience 24 hours of sunlight.

THE AXIAL TILT OF THE EARTH

North ... Rotatio...
Axial Tilt
...ial Pole
...tial Equator
...cliptic

Wobble, Wobble

Earth's tilt is hard to miss. Ancient astronomers knew about it more than 3,000 years ago! What's harder to spot is its wobble, ever so slight, as it dips about 20 feet (6 m) and returns to its original position every 435 days like a top about to topple over. Lots of factors—the gravitational tug of the moon and sun, the movement of the Earth's interior, or even waves pushing across the ocean—might cause the wobble. It has become a puzzle for astronomers and a hassle for global-positioning satellites, which is why the wobble is a relatively new discovery!

What if Earth didn't have a moon?

Roughly 140 natural satellites, called moons, orbit the planets in our solar system, but there's only one known simply as "the moon." Earth's sole satellite is literally a chip off the old block, formed around 4.5 billion years ago when a Mars-size planet named Theia collided with the infant Earth and blasted debris into orbit. The debris encircled the planet as a ring of rock before scrunching down to form the moon.

Since ancient times, the moon has loomed large in human history. Its orbit around Earth inspired our calendar month. Its gravitational pull coaxes Earth's seas into daily cycles of high and low tides. Over billions of years, the moon's "tidal pull" on our planet slowed its rotation; without the moon, our day would only last six to eight hours instead of 24. Scientists even suspect that our satellite's stabilizing effect on Earth's wobble and climates helped life evolve here. Without the moon, there might not have been humans around to appreciate solar eclipses—which, incidentally, we also wouldn't have without a moon.

Good Night, Moon

Just as Earth's moon hasn't been around since the beginning, it won't hang around until the end. It's actually drifting away from Earth by a few centimeters every year even as it drags down our planet's rotation (which is why days used to be much shorter in the ancient past). But don't bid goodbye to the moon just yet. It will remain a fixture in Earth's sky for billions of years—longer, even, than the sun will.

123

What if

Seas will rise!
Nations will sink!
Species will go extinct!

From snowy ice ages to worldwide heat waves, Earth's climate has been subject to natural changes throughout its long history. But in the last century or so, the planet's atmosphere has warmed 1.5 degrees Fahrenheit (0.8 degrees Celsius)—mostly since 1960. That's when humans began a surge in their burning of fossil fuels (coal, oil, and natural gas) to power their homes, cars, planes, and factories. (Burning fossil fuels produces carbon dioxide, which occurs naturally in the atmosphere. Animals exhale carbon dioxide, and plants use it for photosynthesis.) But these natural processes absorb only about half of the carbon dioxide produced by burning fossil fuels. The rest of it builds in the atmosphere and traps heat from the sun, which is why it's called a greenhouse gas. At the rate that human activity is pumping this stuff out, Earth's atmosphere could heat up as much as 7.2 degrees Fahrenheit (4 degrees Celsius) by the end of this century. What will happen if we don't cool it?

MELTING POLAR REGIONS COULD LEAVE ANIMALS VYING FOR SPACE.

Sinking Feeling

An increase in worldwide heat will lead to more than just extra-sticky summers. Like ice cubes left in an unplugged freezer, the world's glaciers will thaw and run off into streams and oceans. Warmer air, meanwhile, causes seawater to expand. The result: Sea levels will rise between 7 and 23 inches (18 and 59 cm) by the end of this century—more if the ice over land at the South Pole continues to melt into the ocean. Rising waters will flood wetlands and other delicate coastal habitats, wiping out species. Among them: humans. About 40 percent of the world's population lives within 60 miles (100 km) of the sea, mostly in low-lying floodplains and towns and cities. Entire nations will be swallowed by the sea if their leaders don't make plans now. The president of the Indian Ocean nation of Maldives has suggested using tourist dollars to buy a new country—one safely above the rising sea level.

Side Effects Include ...

FREAKY FORECAST

Weather in a warming world will be more difficult to predict and more dangerous. Extreme storms such as hurricanes and tornadoes will become stronger and more common. Higher sea levels will cause more flooding in coastal areas, while longer dry seasons and droughts will lead to wildfires and starvation from wiped-out crops.

TROUBLED WATERS

Although ocean levels will rise, the world's supply of freshwater will actually drop. The Quelccaya Ice Cap in Peru—a source of water and electricity for thousands of people—could be gone by the turn of the century. Newly created wetlands in other areas, meanwhile, will become breeding grounds for mosquitoes, spreading killer diseases such as malaria.

CREATURE DISCOMFORTS

Changing climates will throw entire wildlife ecosystems out of whack. It's already happening. Some butterflies, foxes, and plants have moved north to find cooler habitats. Species that depend on these animals for food will need to find new sources or go extinct. The most famous example is the polar bear—a species that is already feeling the heat. If the ice in the Arctic Circle disappears, so will the bears.

Planet Hacks: Drastic Tactics for Reversing Climate Change

If reducing carbon emissions isn't enough to halt the Earth's rising temperatures, scientists are dreaming up plans B, C, and D: planetwide "geoengineering" schemes to cool the climate artificially. For instance ...

Space-Based Sunblocks: Rockets will carry trillions of reflective discs millions of miles into Earth orbit to block the sunlight, sort of like a colossal pair of sunglasses.

Carbon Dioxide Removers: Nations will restore vast tracts of forest on land and spur plankton growth in the ocean to boost the processes that scrub carbon dioxide from the atmosphere.

Atmospheric Effects: Taking a cue from massive volcanic eruptions that cool the planet with their high-altitude ash flows, scientists will seed the stratosphere with special particles designed to reflect sunlight.

Could it Happen???

SOLAR POWER PANELS

In late 2015, 195 countries reached an agreement to reduce the amount of greenhouse gases they're pumping into the atmosphere. The deal involves focusing on renewable sources of energy, such as solar and wind power, and using technologies to capture and store carbon dioxide spewed out by factories and fossil-fuel power plants. Scientists don't believe the agreement is enough to halt a jump in global temperatures of 2 degrees Celsius (or 3.6 degrees Fahrenheit)—the point of no return before we face an increase in the calamities mentioned above—but it's a start. People can do their part by embracing "smart" technologies that rely on sensors to power their homes efficiently, but the real challenge will be convincing the oil, gas, and coal companies to leave the fossil fuels in the ground and switch to renewable energy sources. This would require the companies to sacrifice massive profits for the good of the planet, so it would likely require the outcry of millions and government intervention.

What if

The night (and day) sky would rock—with a ring of dull rocks instead of shiny ice ...

As you read earlier in this chapter, the Earth did have rings at one point, but they weren't like Saturn's famous rings, and no humans were around to spy them in the sky. In fact, life on Earth didn't even exist yet. About 4.5 billion years ago, a small planet smashed into the Earth and blasted trillions of tons of debris into orbit that eventually bunched up to form our moon. But before that big crunch, the debris spread across the sky to create rings of rock around our world. What if those rings never went away?

Rousing Rubble

The only way the rings would've stayed is if they had formed much closer to Earth—within something called the "Roche limit." Named for the 19th-century French mathematician Édouard Roche who calculated it, the Roche limit is the zone of space around the Earth in which passing heavenly bodies are pulverized by our planet's gravity. Because the ring of debris was blasted above the Roche limit, it was able to form into the moon. Had it fallen within the Roche limit, the debris would have remained as rings of rubble around Earth's Equator, visible from nearly every spot on the planet.

To ring watchers living on the Equator, the rubble above wouldn't be much to look at: just a skinny belt of brown stretching from horizon to horizon directly overhead. The rings would become more visible as you travel farther north or south of the Equator. They would reflect the sunlight, just as the moon's surface does, but the show wouldn't be quite as awe-inspiring as the one put on by Saturn's famous belt. Saturn's rings are made of ice as well as rock, glittering like a sheet of diamonds. Sunsets seen through Earth's dusty rings might make up for its lack of luster. Intensely red, they would be out of this world.

TELESCOPES ON TOP OF MAUNA KEA IN HAWAII, U.S.A.

Side Effects Include ...

A CATASTROPHIC COLLISION MIGHT CREATE A RING.

ROCKET BLOCKER

Space agencies like NASA build their launch facilities closer to the Equator to take advantage of Earth's faster rotation there, which gives rockets and shuttles a speed boost into orbit. But that ring of debris overhead would make launches and orbital maneuvers much trickier and riskier. Navigating Earth's rings of rubble, in fact, would be even more dangerous than traveling through the asteroid belt.

LAUNCH OF ATLAS V FROM CAPE CANAVERAL

COOL EFFECTS

Not only would Earth cast a creepy shadow—visible at night—on the rings up above, but the rings would cast a shadow on the Earth down below. Tropical regions that fell under that shadow in the winter months would become a little extra chilly.

SKYWAY ROBBERY

Astronomers across the world would have a more difficult time studying the heavens with a fat ring of rock blocking a portion of their view. To study the heavens properly, they would need to build observatories closer to the North or South Poles, where the ring would be less obtrusive.

Could it Happen?

Earth's moon is safely above the Roche limit—and that's a good thing! As you learned earlier in this chapter, the moon and its gravitational effect on our planet's wobble and tides may have helped nurture the spread of life on Earth. A ring, on the other hand, would lack the moon's gravitational pull, which means no tides and possibly no life.

But that doesn't mean we'll never see a ring around our world. After all, three other planets in our solar system besides Saturn—Jupiter, Uranus, and Neptune—have them, formed from bits of asteroids and comets that were captured by their powerful gravity and pulverized into rings within their respective Roche limits. A similar heavenly body could zip in Earth's direction, get caught by its gravity within the Roche limit, and become slowly ground into a beautiful ring system made of rock and ice. Of course, it's far more likely such an object would simply smash into the planet and cause devastation on a global scale, which is why we should just be happy with our ring-free sky.

What if

Suddenly, 97 percent of Earth's once hidden living space is yours to explore!

Now you see the sea. Glug, glug, glug. Now you don't. We've just emptied 321,000,000 cubic miles—or cubes that measure one mile on each of their sides (1,338,000,000 cubic km)—of seawater from every ocean on the planet. In an instant, terrain that would have taken 125 years to map by ship is suddenly exposed to the sky. Scientists know more about the far side of the moon than they do the bottom of the ocean, so this is your big chance to peel back the waves and visit the sea's most stunning sights—no submarine required (although you will need some climbing gear).

EVEREST BUSTER
Mauna Kea, Hawaii, U.S.A.

Let's start with Mauna Kea, a volcano that rises 13,680 feet (4,170 m) above the island of Hawaii. With the Pacific Ocean now empty, this monster mountain stands more than 30,000 feet (9,144 m) from its base to its summit, taller than Mount Everest.

SHEER BEAUTY
Great Bahamas Bank

You wouldn't know it when you snorkel in the clear waters of the Bahamas, but these Caribbean islands are home to the highest cliffs on the planet. The Great Bahama Bank begins right where the sea shifts from light blue to near black. That color shift makes sense now that the water's gone: The islands' edges are actually cliffs rising two miles (3.2 km) above a sprawling plain.

GRANDER CANYON
Monterey Bay, California, U.S.A.

With the ocean emptied, Arizona's Grand Canyon is no longer the only chasm that lives up to its name. A network of chasms off California's coast is just as awe-inspiring and nearly the same size. It's far from the largest canyon in the ocean. A series of canyons in the Bering Sea is large enough to swallow this one. While canyons on land are carved out by rivers and wind, undersea canyons have more mysterious origins. According to one theory, they were formed by underwater avalanches.

SUNKEN TREASURES
Everywhere

History's most mysterious sunken cities—Cleopatra's lost palace off Egypt, the pirate stronghold of Port Royal in Jamaica, and perhaps even the lost city of Atlantis—are suddenly back on the map. Lost ships from across the centuries now drip-dry in the sunlight. The irony is that these wooden and iron artifacts will quickly crumble to dust in the open air unless they're stored in seawater for safekeeping. In this world of empty oceans, only aquariums and museums will have seawater.

Could it Happen?

Draining the ocean to explore its archaeological treasures and geological wonders comes at a steep price: An Earth without seas is a lousy place to live. Plants and algae in the ocean produce half of the oxygen we breathe and absorb nearly one-third of the carbon dioxide that is causing a gradual heating of the planet. Oceans are also home to an incredible abundance of life. The variety of creatures in the deep sea alone rivals the diversity of rain forests on land. Oceans are a crucial piece of the system that drives weather, winds, and local climates. On second thought, you're better off leaving their drain plug in place. (Besides, where would all that water go?)

ROCK BOTTOM
Challenger Deep in the Pacific Ocean

Hundreds of people climb Everest each year, but only two people have touched bottom in the world's deepest spot, the Challenger Deep, which sits below nearly seven miles (11 km) of water in the Pacific Ocean's Mariana Trench. Now you can hike to the bottom of a trench that yesterday was in perpetual darkness. Just watch your step around the pools of liquid sulfur and geysers of molten mud.

Chapter 7:
Worst-Case Scenarios

By this point in the book, you've experimented with stupendous superpowers, chatted with dolphins through a translating device, and explored a parallel world in which the dinosaurs never died. That's a pretty good run of fun adventures, but now it's time to get serious. Brace yourself for a chapter of real buzzkills: the parachute that doesn't open, the sailboat that capsizes at sea, the rock that streaks in from space, and other very bad what-if scenarios that you'll only want to find between the covers of this book.

What if aliens invaded Earth?

WARNING

This chapter may freak you out, but don't worry, we'll explain how—and why—you'll be fine!

What if you were struck with amnesia?

What if you stepped in lava?

What Would Happen If...

What if

Don't panic! People have survived miles-high plummets.

Imagine you've just leapt from a plane at 12,000 feet (3,658 m) and realized you forgot one important detail: your parachute! (Such a scary scenario is extremely unlikely—skydiving professionals follow rigorous pre-jump checks—but it has happened!) Gravity is now your greatest enemy as it tugs you toward the turf below. Air, on the other hand, is your best buddy. Atmospheric resistance cushions your body and counteracts gravity's pull, putting a speed limit on your descent at around 120 miles an hour (193 km/h). You reach this "terminal velocity" about 12 seconds after stepping out of the plane. What you do next will determine your odds of surviving your rendezvous with the soil.

Keeping a Positive Altitude

Believe it or not, things could be worse. You have time on your side! People who tumble from big bridges or tall buildings hit the ground in mere seconds. If you spread your arms and legs to create the maximum amount of atmospheric drag (make like a flying squirrel!), you'll have more than a minute to plan your landing. Scan the landscape below for the softest spots. Fine details will be hard to see from way up here, so look for places where you *don't* want to touch down: parking lots, roads, and even lakes and seas. Belly flops sting for a reason: Water doesn't squish into itself like air or that foam in your bubble bath. Plummeting into the sea from a great height would be no better than slamming into a driveway.

Water in the form of snow, on the other hand, makes the safest landing zone. Drifts of snow are the best—especially if you can aim to roll down a snowy hillside—so scan for fresh powder as you fall. Swamps are the next best thing. That goopy muck has a lot of give. If you don't see any swampland, aim for a forest.

Branches have broken the falls of out-of-control sky-divers in the past. Tin roofs, glass skylights, and even high-tension wires will help you bleed speed before your inevitable reunion with Earth's surface. Once you've picked your landing spot, veer for it by pointing your head in its direction and tucking up your arms. You should be able to soar at least a mile in any direction as you fall if you start steering early.

The ground is rushing up quickly now. You can make out individual trees, sidewalks, people, and cars (which aren't a bad landing spot, either; car roofs crumple on impact). It's time to prepare for landing. Break out of your flying-squirrel posture and lock your arms to your sides. The United States Federal Aviation Administration recommends landing feet first with your legs together and your heels up. Keep your knees and hips flexed and try to collapse sideways to absorb the shock of impact. Keep a cool head and follow all these steps. And don't forget your parachute next time!

FLYING SQUIRREL

Side Effects Include ...

INTO THIN AIR

Falling from a greater height—say, the six-mile (9.7-km) altitude flown by passenger planes—would have given you more time, but the air way up there is so thin you would have passed out from a lack of oxygen, only to wake up to see the ground rushing up at you. That would have left you with even less time to prepare!

FEARSOME TEARS

Falling at 120 miles an hour (193 km/h) is like sticking your head out the window of a bullet train: The force of the wind would fill your eyes with blinding tears. That's why skydiving goggles are the second most important piece of equipment after your parachute. Without them, you wouldn't be able to scan the ground for the safest place to land.

FREE FALL

Could it Happen?

Not only could this scenario happen—it *has* happened: more than a dozen times according to the Free Fall Research Page, an online record of people who survived all sorts of high-altitude tumbles to the ground. Among the lucky survivors was Nicholas Alkemade, who leapt from his blasted-to-bits British bomber in World War II and fell 18,000 feet (5,486 m). His fall was broken by tree branches, brush, and drifts of snow. He survived with just an injured knee and some cuts and bruises. In 1993, a New Zealand skydiver named Klint Freemantle fell 3,600 feet (1,097 m) after both his parachute and emergency parachute failed. Onlookers—including his sister and father—feared the worst when he splashed into a marshy duck pond, but Freemantle walked away from the accident with just a cut over his left eye.

What if

the Yellowstone **supervolcano** had a **super-eruption**?

It would be bad ... but not end-of-the-world bad.

Millions of tourists flock to Yellowstone National Park in Wyoming, U.S.A., to snap photos of its gurgling hot springs and gasp at the world's largest concentration of geysers, the most famous of which, Old Faithful, blasts super-heated water vapor up to 185 feet (56 m) high every 92 minutes. But this awe-inspiring gallery of geological activity is powered by one of the most destructive forces on the planet. Yellowstone sits above a volcano larger than the state of Rhode Island. Known as the Yellowstone Caldera, it blew its top 640,000 years ago, and 660,000 years before that, and 800,000 years before that. According to that schedule, it's due to have another so-called super-eruption any century now. Human beings weren't around the last time Yellowstone exploded. What if it happened tomorrow?

Blast Off

Of the nearly 2,000 active volcanoes across the world, only a handful are considered "super-volcanoes," or capable of eruptions reaching an 8 or more on the Volcanic Explosivity Index. Geologists use this scale to measure the might of a volcano's explosive eruption and the amount of gases, ashes, bits of gas, and rock it would hurl miles into the sky. The 1815 eruption of Mount Tambora on the island of Sumbawa in Indonesia measured a 7, creating a shock wave that was heard up to 1,200 miles (2,000 km) away and spewing ash into the atmosphere for the next three years. It was the most powerful eruption on Earth in 10,000 years, and yet it was not considered a supervolcano. A super-eruption of the Yellowstone Caldera would be a thousand times more powerful.

Fifteen miles (24 km) below Yellowstone hides a reservoir of molten rock—or magma—that wells up from below and could fill the Grand Canyon to the brim again and again and again. As the magma nears the top of the chamber, it undergoes chemical reactions that squeeze out the less-dense materials, such as water, gases, and a glasslike substance called silica. This hot mix bubbles against the top of the magma chamber, which contains immense pressures, like a soda can kicked around a parking lot at high noon. These forces heave against the ground, causing it to rise and then fall as pressure is released through Yellowstone's hot springs, bubbling mud pots, steam vents, and famous geysers.

But if the gases and silica concentrations in this subterranean pressure cooker expand too quickly,

Side Effects Include ...

SUN DOWN

The eruption of Mount Tambora in 1815 spewed ash into the atmosphere for the next three years, blocking the sun and lowering global temperatures. Crops across the world withered, and tens of thousands of people died from famine. A massive eruption of the Yellowstone Caldera might lock the planet in a similar "volcanic winter" that could affect agriculture for many years.

LAVA FLOW

SLO-MO FLOW

Instead of a super-eruption, the Yellowstone Caldera is much more likely to have a "nonexplosive" eruption that produces lava flows. These rivers of magma would create a mess in Yellowstone but wouldn't endanger many lives. These types of eruptions are much more common than the last super-eruption that happened 640,000 years ago. In fact, about 80 of these lava-spewing eruptions have happened since then.

BEST WORST-CASE SCENARIO

Scientists with the U.S. Geological Survey are quick to point out that even a super-eruption wouldn't spell doom for humanity. Previous super-eruptions didn't lead to mass extinctions or cause much fallout on the fringes of the continent. Modern conveniences we take for granted would likely disappear for a while. The umbrella-shaped plume of ash, thousands of miles across, would throw rescue efforts into chaos, shutting down communication and air travel across the United States for about a year.

the Yellowstone Caldera literally blows its top, unleashing an explosion that would launch more than 240 cubic miles (1,000 cubic km) of ash, mud, rock, and splinters of glass into the sky. Nearby states would be buried beneath up to three feet (1 m) of ash, heavy enough to smash buildings. A layer of this choking ash would reach most parts of the United States. Closer to the park, avalanches of ash and gas that reach more than 1000°F (537°C) in the blink of an eye would hurtle from the crater at hurricane-force speeds. Anyone caught in one of these "pyroclastic" flows would be doomed.

Could it Happen?

Breathe easy. Despite what some news reports and click-hungry websites might claim, the Yellowstone Caldera is not overdue for a catastrophic eruption. According to scientists monitoring the caldera from their station in the park, the chances of a Yellowstone super-eruption are extremely slim—as in a 1-in-730,000 chance. It may never have a massive eruption again. It's far more likely that the Yellowstone volcano would have a nonexplosive event that would just flood the park with lava (and even these events are rare). Any super-eruption would be preceded by all sorts of earthquakes and other geological activity, giving us months or even years to prepare.

What if aliens invaded Earth?

We should just pretend we're not home and hope they leave us alone.

Previously in this book, we pondered what would happen if astronomers found alien life on another planet in our solar system or beyond. Such a discovery would change everything, from how we explore space to the way we see ourselves as Earthlings. But not everyone is ready to welcome E.T. with open arms. Physicist Stephen Hawking, a true believer in alien life, believes we better do everything we can to hide from extraterrestrial astronauts. He fears that alien invaders would ransack Earth for its resources or colonize it. Earthlings would be enslaved or, worse, wiped out. Hawking is regarded as the most brilliant scientific mind since Albert Einstein. What if he's right?

Space Invaders

Humans haven't explored our own solar system well enough to rule out the presence of brainy extraterrestrials in our own backyard. "Perhaps if we someday explore the asteroid belt we might find evidence of mining or the waste products of an extraterrestrial industry," says astrobiologist Jacob Haqq-Misra. "But the much more likely case is that Earth is the only inhabited planet in the solar system, and [intelligent extraterrestrial] life might exist on planets orbiting other stars." Any aliens that can pay us a visit from outside our solar system would possess technology light-years ahead of our own. After all, these travelers have figured out how to cross the vast distances between stars. Here on Earth, the invention of the airplane is barely more than a century old.

If alien visitors were bent on giving us a hard time, we'd be as helpless as ants trying to battle a bully with a magnifying glass. And like these ants, our best chance for survival might be to burrow deep underground and hope the mean kid loses interest. "Humans could probably put up a fight with some of our technology," says Haqq-Misra, "but if the [extraterrestrial intelligence] is advanced enough, there's little we could do." As sci-fi author Arthur C. Clarke once said, "Any sufficiently advanced technology is indistinguishable from magic."

FRIEND OR FOE?

SETI STATION

In Case of **Close Encounters ...**

Back in 1996, the Search for Extraterrestrial Intelligence—or SETI project—came up with a step-by-step guide—complete with a serious-sounding title, the "Post-Detection SETI Protocol"—in case E.T. decided to phone Earth ...

Step 1: **Check the signal**

If a SETI station picks up a mysterious radio signal, it's the station's job to confirm that the signal really is from deep space and verify it with other SETI experts. No point in getting everyone on Earth excited about a radio glitch.

Step 2: **Tell the world**

In movies, evidence of alien life is always swept under the rug by government agents. SETI's plan is to share the news with the world—through the scientific community—as soon as the signal is confirmed as legit.

Step 3: **Clear the airwaves**

Radio operators across the globe will halt broadcasting on whatever frequencies carry the alien signal. This way scientists can monitor the broadcast without interference. They will try to determine whether the signal is a direct message to us Earthlings or just the background buzz of an ancient extraterrestrial civilization.

Step 4: **Call back ... maybe**

After learning as much as possible about the alien civilization—such as whether they might be friends or foes—scientists from around the world, members of the United Nations, and other experts will decide if it's safe to broadcast a greeting from Earth. It might take our message dozens, hundreds, or even thousands of years to reach the source of the alien signal, but it would eventually let them know right where we live. Some scientists don't think that's worth the risk of an unfriendly visit.

TAKING A STROLL

Don't bother trying to impress our alien overlords with your smartphone or your latest Xbox game system. Our technology will seem primitive to any alien invaders. They're probably here for Earth's resources: water, metals, minerals, and possibly its life-forms for lunch. "I do wonder if humans might be a delicacy for E.T.s seeking exotic foods," says Haqq-Misra. "Would humans be a rare treat like truffles? A health food that alien kids hate?"

See next page for more!

What's in it for them?

Astrobiologist Jacob Haqq-Misra weighs in on why aliens might attack ...

EARTHLING NUGGETS?

"The idea that [an extraterrestrial intelligence] would want to eat us because of hunger seems extremely unlikely. Any civilization that has mastered the ability to travel interstellar distances must certainly have already solved any problems relating to food production."

A REST STOP?

"[Intelligent extraterrestrials] might go planet to planet, stripping each of its resources and then moving on. But such intelligent extraterrestrials would be very short-lived on timescales compared to the [age of the] galaxy, so there probably aren't too many of them left."

Side Effects of an Alien Invasion Include ...

COSMIC ACCIDENT

The Spanish conquest of the New World in the 15th century spread smallpox, a highly contagious disease that killed more than a third of the Native American population. Some scientists fear that extraterrestrial visitors would bring a similar illness, accidentally wiping out the human race.

SHOW OF FORCE

Instead of enslaving Earthlings or harvesting our planet's resources, intelligent aliens might drop by for another reason: entertainment. "Humans keep animals in captivity for abilities that are fairly silly or benign, such as seals that balance balls on their noses, or lions that can jump through hoops," says Haqq-Misra. "Perhaps [extraterrestrial intelligence] would find similar amusement purposes for humans?"

EARTHLING ENTERTAINMENT

Could it Happen?

Taking the universe's old age (13.4 billion years old!) and its vast size (trillions of planets in billions of galaxies!) into account, a physicist named Enrico Fermi calculated that our own Milky Way galaxy ought to be teeming with intelligent life. By that logic, Earth should be bathed in radio transmissions—interplanetary emails, ship-to-ship communications, otherworldly sitcoms—from across the galaxy. And yet astronomers have failed to detect any signals from distant worlds. Called the Fermi paradox, this radio silence from space has some scientists convinced that we are alone in the universe. But not all scientists. "To declare that Earth must be the only planet with life in the universe would be inexcusably bigheaded of us," writes astrophysicist Neil deGrasse Tyson in his book *Death by Black Hole*.

If the thought of alien invaders keeps you awake at night, then the Fermi paradox should help you catch up on your z's. But some scientists theorize that advanced alien civilizations communicate with technology that we can't detect, or that an advanced extraterrestrial culture would scan Earth and determine that it harbors no intelligent life—at least not an intelligence worth their time. "If the [extraterrestrials] are vastly more advanced than us," says Haqq-Misra, "then perhaps they already visit us from time to time without us ever knowing. Do ants know when we pass by their anthill?"

Regardless of the possibilities of intelligent alien life—friend or foe—it's too late for us to lie low and hope no one out there notices us. We've been broadcasting our position through radio shows, then TV programs, and now cell-phone conversations for nearly one hundred years. If any advanced alien societies live within a hundred light-years of Earth, they already know we're here.

PEOPLE POWER?

"The same logic [behind using Earthlings for food] applies to using us as labor. I suspect that most laborious tasks would be automated by robots."

FRIENDS IN HIGH PLACES

Alien visitors are just as likely to be friends as foes. They might be monitoring Earthlings even now, waiting for us to achieve some technological or social milestone before dropping by to share their secrets for exploring the universe. That is, if they don't accidentally wipe us out with some alien germs first.

Doomsday Scenarios

"ROGUE" COMET

What if an asteroid was on a crash course with Earth?

Nobody knows when the next large asteroid—such as the one that created the moon or wiped out the dinosaurs—will head toward our home planet, but the consequences could be catastrophic. Seas will boil. Forests will burn. Cities will crumble. Clouds of choking ash will smother the planet. Entire species—perhaps even humans—will go extinct.

Asteroids travel at tens of thousands of miles an hour, speeds that transfer into destructive energy when they collide with a planet, moon, or each other. A single rock at least 450 feet (138 m) across could destroy an entire city. More than a thousand people were injured in 2013 when an asteroid just 62 feet (19 m) wide exploded high in the atmosphere above Chelyabinsk, Russia. And that was a near miss!

In 2013, NASA announced its Asteroid Grand Challenge to locate any nasty asteroids heading our way and prevent their impact. Rock-stopping strategies include melting the incoming asteroid with a space-based laser, splattering it with white paint that would turn the surface into a sail for solar radiation to push it off course, and using the gravitational pull of a large spaceship to "tug" an asteroid off its collision course with Earth. And if none of those options work, space agencies can always resort to brute force: ramming the asteroid with a rocket to knock it back to space.

Comet Cleansers

Rocks aren't the only rogue bodies roaming the solar system. Comets originate far out in the solar system—some from the Kuiper belt of icy bodies beyond the orbit of Neptune, and others from a more distant region known as the Oort cloud. Each is an irregular ball of icy slush, frozen gases, and dark minerals just a few miles or kilometers wide. But like asteroids, comets occasionally collide with planets (one slammed into Jupiter in 1994) and have the potential to cause calamity.

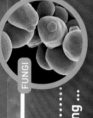

PARASITE

VIRUS

BACTERIA

FUNGI

What if a deadly disease spread across the globe?

One of the biggest threats to our survival is an enemy too small to see with the naked eye: germs. Deadly bacteria and viruses—in the form of widespread infectious outbreaks known as pandemics—have killed more people throughout history than all wars combined. A plague known as the Black Death killed one out of three people in Europe in the 14th century. A flu pandemic in 1918 killed as many as 100 million people around the world. Pandemics tend to happen every 10 to 50 years. We're overdue for the next one.

Immunizations and advances in medicine protect us from these diseases but can also put us at risk. Scientists fear that overuse of antibiotics—medications that kill dangerous bacteria—is responsible for the rise in "superbugs": germs that resist antibiotics. A superbug spread

through coughing or physical contact could ravage a city in weeks. Modern air travel means such a disease could spread across the world in months. But have hope: Even an especially deadly pandemic wouldn't wipe out the world's entire population of roughly seven billion. Some people have a natural immunity—or resistance—to the illness. Isolated towns and island nations could quarantine themselves from the disease's ill effects. Humans have recovered from terrifying pandemics in the past. We could do it again.

Meet the Little Monsters

The term "germ" encompasses an army of tiny terrors, including ...

Bacteria: Blame sore throats, ear infections, and tooth-tartar buildup on these single-celled organisms. They create microscopic poops that can act as a poison inside the host.

Viruses: Most viruses are frail things (unlike bacteria and fungi, viruses aren't even alive) that can only replicate inside a host. Colds, flus, chicken pox, immune disorders, and measles are all caused by viruses.

Fungi: These microscopic molds, yeasts, and other plantlike pathogens thrive in wet, warm places like our armpits, belly buttons, and the spaces between our toes. They produce stinky wastes that irritate our skin.

Parasites: This ghastly germ group includes itty-bitty insect larvae, amoebas, and one-celled organisms called protozoa that sneak into our bodies in tainted water and food, causing us all sorts of gastrointestinal gripes.

What if

you **stepped** in **lava**?

Ouch! Ouch! Ouch!
You better be fast on your feet!

We've all tried this playground game: Everyone pretends the ground is covered with a lake of searing lava. Players leap from tree stumps to sidewalks to the rungs on the jungle gym in a race to save their soles from an imaginary scorching. Last one to land in the lava wins! But what would happen if you lost the lava game in real life? Your odds of saving your feet from this risky feat depend on the type of hot rock you walk on.

Earth's crust rides on massive plates floating on a sea of molten—or hot liquid—rock called magma, which is known as lava when it bubbles to the surface through undersea vents or one of nearly 2,000 active volcanoes wherever two plates meet. In "effusive" volcanoes, the lava flows at a steady rate, often forming new mountains and islands (which is how the islands of Hawaii, U.S.A., were formed). Lava that flows from volcanoes and vents can reach 2000°F (1100°C)—hot enough to melt anything in its path.

Hot Foot

As far as molten rock that oozes from the Earth goes, pahoehoe lava (a Hawaiian word pronounced paw-hoey-hoey) is the only type that might work for a real-life lava game. It usually flows slowly enough (in thin clumps called tongues) for people to outpace it at walking speed. More importantly, pahoehoe lava's top layer cools into a thin skin of rock that blocks the intense heat of its red-hot interior. Without this protective skin, pahoehoe would heat the air around like an oven, setting fire to trees and melting any aluminum jungle gyms you tried to climb during the lava game. Even with its skin, pahoehoe is hot enough to make the air above it shimmer. You wipe the sweat from your forehead as you approach the flow from upwind. You brace against the heat. Gently, you

take a step on the molten rock, bracing to sink into a searing mush.

Well, this is unexpected—the lava feels almost solid! Pressing down barely dents it. Keep applying pressure, however, and you'll break the protective skin. Uh-oh! Flames and heat flare up around your foot. Retreat! Linger and your sneakers will burst into flames, followed by your foot and everything attached to it. You back carefully away from the pahoehoe flow (again, staying upwind) and be careful not to touch it or you'll wind up with third-degree burns!

Side Effects Include ...

SPONTANEOUS COMBUSTION

You definitely don't want to trip and slip into any molten rock. Movies make falling into lava look like a deadly dive into a flaming pool. If you fell into lava in real life, you wouldn't actually sink. Lava is much denser than water, so you would just sort of float on the top and burst into flames. If you accidentally tumbled into an active volcano's crater, you would catch fire before you even hit the lava's surface.

EXCESSIVE DRESS

Unless you want the soles of your shoes turning to goo, you'll need appropriate attire for your lava trot. Geologist Erik Klemetti recommends something like snowshoes to help spread your weight across the lava's skin, except with thick soles made of a flame-resistant material to keep your tootsies from toasting. The hottest fashion for lava living is a "fire-proximity suit" insulated to protect against the extreme temperatures. Hey, you look good in silver!

Could it Happen?

Hawaiian hiking guides and daredevil volcanologists (people who study volcanoes) have stepped on lava and walked home to post their videos on the Internet. (There's an entire video channel online featuring people chucking objects—from ordinary rocks to canned ravioli—into lava.) At least two volcanologists in Hawaii have accidentally fallen into molten rock and required a trip to the hospital to treat their burns. Both survived.

FIRE-PROXIMITY SUIT

What if you were lost at sea?

A shipwreck survivor shares his scary experience ...

One minute it's smooth sailing. And then ... crash! A rogue wave—or perhaps a piece of flotsam or even a rogue whale—has cracked the hull of your boat. It's taking on water fast. Abandon ship! Now you're adrift in a tiny life raft in the middle of the raging ocean. Your pleasure cruise has become a nightmare.

American sailor Steve Callahan knows the feeling. He drifted in a small raft for 76 days in the Atlantic Ocean after his sailboat sank (possibly because of a whale attack) during a windy night in 1981. By the time he reached rescue off the coast of Guadalupe Island, Callahan had drifted 1,800 miles (2,897 km) and lost a third of his body weight to hunger and thirst. And now you get to join him during his perilous journey adrift ...

INFLATABLE LIFE RAFT

The Moment of Impact

"As the boat was going down, I heard a voice inside of me screaming and panicking," Callahan says, "but then another part started telling me to just shut [up] and do what had to be done." A veteran sailor, Callahan knew he needed to stock his life raft with enough stuff to survive for weeks at sea—or longer. He dove again and again into the flooded hold of his sinking sailboat to retrieve essential items, including a soggy sleeping bag, a speargun, two solar stills that converted seawater to drinking water, a pump for his raft, and an emergency kit before the boat began drifting away. He was 800 miles (1,287 km) from land in a six-foot (1.8-m)-wide inflatable raft with only a tarp for shade from the punishing sun. "It all felt so strange that I wondered if I was in a dream," Callahan says. "But on the other hand, it couldn't be any more real. I was like, 'Now what?'"

Managing Disasters

Instead of curling up and hoping a passing ship would pluck him to safety, Callahan immediately snapped into survival mode, which meant dealing with a growing list of potentially deadly problems. "When you're going through any crisis—whether it's battling cancer or that your boat just sank in the middle of the ocean—you should *not* obsess too much on the final goal," Callahan says. "What you're really focusing on is the immediate step: What you're doing right now. You divvy the survival experiences into achievable chunks." Callahan knew he would soon die of exposure if he didn't warm his body, so he wrapped himself in the wet sleeping bag. His next priority: drinking water. He collected rain and used his glitchy solar stills to collect just enough to survive. He then figured out how to catch fish using his broken speargun and lures made of fish parts while keeping his leaky raft afloat. "Every single day I would prioritize what needed the most attention," he says.

DORADO

Steve Callahan made a full recovery from his ordeal adrift. Today he's an author, a consultant on sea survival for Hollywood movies, and a designer of boats and lifeboats. He still loves the ocean.

Survival Routine

Callahan let his hopes soar whenever he spotted a ship on the horizon during his first two weeks adrift. He was sure he attracted the attention of one after firing off signal flares, but the vessel continued on and disappeared. Eventually, as Callahan drifted farther into the Atlantic, the ships stopped appearing altogether. "I couldn't count on the hope that I'd be picked up," he says. "I knew I could only count on myself." To keep from sinking into despair, Callahan tried to follow his ordinary shipboard routine despite the extraordinary circumstances. He would check the weather, log his position using homemade navigational instruments, and exercise as much as possible in the tiny raft—which he had named the *Rubber Ducky*. "I tried to conjure the idea that this wasn't the end of a voyage but just a continuation in a much more humble craft," he says.

Fishing Buddies

Callahan may have been sailing solo, but he still had companions for the trip. A small community of sea creatures—sleek dorado fish and the occasional curious shark—began skulking beneath the *Rubber Ducky*. At first they kept a safe distance from Callahan. As he studied them with a mixture of fascination and hope, he noticed the dorado darting within range of his speargun. He began catching them for food, which attracted a squadron of hungry seabirds over the raft. When one of the speared fish rammed the raft with its exposed spear tip, Callahan used his quick wits to save the *Rubber Ducky* from sinking. The hovering seabirds eventually attracted a boat of fishermen, who thought the birds might signal a school of fish. Instead, they found Callahan—skinny, weak, and battered by the elements. After 76 days alone in the Atlantic, he had been rescued. "Those fish provided me with sustenance," says Callahan. "They became my friends, they almost killed me, and in the end they brought me my salvation."

What if

Things would get worse before they got better.

When you switch on the lights tonight or hop on the bus to school tomorrow, spare a thought for the plants and animals that lived—and died—hundreds of millions of years ago. Their decomposing bodies spent the ages buried deep underground, squeezed by the intense heat and pressures of the Earth until they boiled down into deposits of oil, coal, and natural gas. Mining companies then dug up these "fossil fuels" and refined them into energy sources: electricity for your lights, heat for your house, and fuel for your family's car. Today, fossil fuels meet most of the world's energy needs. But you can probably guess why they're called nonrenewable energy: Someday they'll run out. What if that someday was today?

GRASSHOPPER OIL PUMPS

Dark Age

Without a doubt, nearly every nation on Earth will have a lousy afternoon when the last dregs of fossil fuels run dry. Oil—refined into gasoline—is the main source of fuel for the world's cars, trucks, and airplanes. Without it, gas gauges will hit E and transportation across the world will grind to a halt. In the United States, where nearly 70 percent of electricity is generated by coal and natural gas, entire cities and stretches of the countryside will plunge into a cold, dark night. Internet networks will go down. Air-conditioners and central heat will shut off. Smart-phones and HDTV screens will fade to black.

But within this sea of darkness will shine islands of light. Cities that depend on nuclear or water-powered energy—about 28 percent of the U.S.—will still have power. Here people with electric cars can plug in their vehicles and still get around. Nations

solar, wind, and geothermal power (the heat from inside the Earth)—will become the new superpowers.

And the rest of the world will follow. In fact, it's already happening, slowly in the United States and more rapidly in other countries. "After decades of work, the costs of renewable sources of energy are now plunging," says NASA scientist Dennis Bushnell. "Because of those lower costs, we are moving to renewable energy." Germany has plugged into the sun in a big way, receiving half of its electricity from solar power. Denmark is leading the world in wind power. Iceland gets much of its power from the heat of the Earth. Unlike with fossil fuels, these sources of renewable energy don't heat the atmosphere with excess carbon dioxide. Unlike the other worst-case scenarios in this chapter, the death of fossil fuels doesn't have an unhappy ending.

Charging Ahead: Light After Fossil Fuels

SOLAR POWER

Sunlight contains ultra-tiny invisible particles called photons that radiate in all directions from the sun's surface. When these photons strike a solar panel, they knock electrons off silicon chips inside. The electrons are directed into an electrical current that travels through wiring to power appliances or feed into batteries for long-term storage. Vast banks of panels spread across plains and lakes can power entire towns. Scientists are also figuring out how to make skyscraper glass—and even street surfaces—out of solar panels.

SOLAR PANELS

WIND POWER

When wind strikes a large fanlike machine called a turbine, it spins propeller blades connected to gears inside the turbine's housing. The gears step up the spin of the blades, so that even a mild breeze results in a rapid spin of a shaft connected to the gears. The shaft turns magnets around a coil of conducting wires—a system known as a generator—to create electrical current. "Wind farms" made of many giant turbines will capture constant breezes to power cities. New turbine-equipped kites may soon harness jet streams: fast-moving rivers of air that course through the atmosphere at the altitudes planes fly.

WIND FARM

SEA POWER

Just as wind turbines can turn trade winds into electricity, marine turbines can harness the motion of the ocean. Equipped with blades just like a wind turbine, these sturdy machines can either sit submerged on the ocean bottom to capture currents or hover at the surface to harness the energy of the tides. Researchers estimate that just one-thousandth of the energy of the Gulf Stream current would supply Florida with 35 percent of its electrical needs.

MARINE TURBINES

ALGAE POWER

So far we've only covered renewable technologies that provide electrical power. What will we put in our cars to make them go (at least the cars that don't have electric motors)? Scientists are pinning their hopes on a saltwater plant known as a halophyte, which can grow cheaply and easily in lakes pumped from the oceans to the world's deserts. Raising crops of this "biofuel" will actually absorb the excess carbon dioxide that's now warming the Earth's atmosphere, making halophyte farming a win-win. By turning living plants into gasoline instead of long-dead fossil fuels, we'll be dragging the world into a bright new age of renewable energy.

ALGAE

Could it Happen?

The good news is we won't run out of fossil fuels any time soon. Mining companies are finding new ways to extract natural gas from the ground and eke even more energy out of dirtier and dirtier types of coal. Oil reserves won't reach their peak until at least 2020. But this news is more of a mixed blessing. New technologies such as chemical-injecting pumps that fracture (or "frack") natural gas from the Earth are bad for the environment. And scientists think we have access to far more fossil-fuel reserves than we can safely burn without releasing a dangerous amount of carbon dioxide into the atmosphere—enough to tip the planet's runaway temperatures past the point of no return. We shouldn't worry about running out of fossil fuels. We need to focus on switching to renewable sources of carbon-free energy before it's too late for the environment.

What if

Wait, who am I? Where am I? What is this book I'm reading?

It's a scene right out of a silly old movie: *conk!* A wallop to the noggin leaves the star unable to recall crucial details of her life—not even her own name! Stricken with amnesia, the victim spends the next 90 minutes of the movie piecing together the past until the most important details reassemble themselves at just the right moment to save the day. Sometimes, all it takes is a second smack to the skull to achieve total recall. And while real-life amnesia doesn't offer all the plot-thickening symptoms of a soap opera, it is a real affliction that can leave those stricken confused, forgetful, and even forgetful that they're forgetful. You don't even need a conk on the head to get it ...

Memory **Blank**

When it comes to retaining memories, your brain is practically a bottomless pit. The source of your astounding powers of recall is a seahorse-shaped slab of tissue called the hippocampus deep inside your brain (actually, you have two of them called hippo-campi). Every time you experience something new—such as when you make a new friend, tackle a new video game, try a new flavor of ice cream, etc.—electrical charges fire through the tissues in your brain, creating chemical links that form a network of pathways out of neurons (or brain cells). Your memories are stored in these connected neurons, and the connections become stronger with repeated exposure to the new experience. When disease, age-related illness, intense emotional shock, or—yes—even a physical blow to the head damages the hippocampi, it can scramble chains of neurons and cause amnesia.

Blast to the Past

But amnesia can come in different forms depending on the type of memory that's damaged versus the kind that's working fine. "Retrograde" amnesia, the sort usually portrayed in movies, is the loss of long-term memories that occurred before the illness or accident: details such as your childhood home, how to tie your shoelaces and speak English, and even your own name. Meanwhile, the short-term memory used to store fleeting information such as the names of people you've just met, an address, or the location of your house keys is functioning normally. If you were stuck with this type of amnesia, you would feel stranded in the present, aware that you had gaps in your past that you needed to fill.

Blast to the Future

"Anterograde" amnesia is much different from the memory loss seen in movies. Victims of this type can remember everything that happened before the accident or disease, but they have trouble forming new memories in the present. An illness or injury has damaged the way the brain transfers short-term memories to long-term ones, leaving the victim trapped in the past and confused about the present. If you were suffering from this type of amnesia, you would have the strange side effect of not realizing you had amnesia. It would be a confusing and even dangerous experience while it lasted. Fortunately for both of these types of memory issues, amnesia usually doesn't last very long.

Could it Happen?

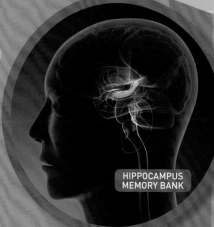

HIPPOCAMPUS MEMORY BANK

Seizures, tumors, surgeries, migraines, whacks to the head—anything that can damage the hippocampus and scramble your neurons can cause amnesia. But this affliction—both the retrograde and anterograde varieties—rarely plays out like the dramatic moments of memory loss in movies. Typical cases of amnesia last just 24 hours. Older memories return first, followed by all of the other details. (And, no, a second blow to the head has never helped anyone recover from amnesia.)

And then there's the case of Henry Gustav Molaison. Born in Louisiana, U.S.A., in 1926, Molaison developed violent seizures after he was hit in the head by a bicycle rider at nine years old. Doctors tried for years to cure his shaking episodes with no effect. Eventually, they resorted to a radical surgery: They removed portions of his hippocampi. For the next 55 years, until his death in 2008, Molaison lived every experience like it was brand new. Imagine hearing every song, trying every dish, and meeting every person like it was the first time! Molaison's severe anterograde amnesia did not affect his memories from before the surgery or his personality. He was a once-in-a-lifetime case—and a crucial patient in the study of memory. His story was like nothing in a movie, and yet it was no less fascinating.

Chapter 8:

REALITY CHUCKED

Your friends have disowned you because you haven't bathed in, like, forever. You dodged an asteroid headed for Earth. By this point in the book, you might be asking "What next?!" instead of "What if?" Well, good news: This final chapter is loaded with nothing but fun situations and absurd scenarios. Think of it as a vacation from the earlier chapter's intense setups—and the perfect way to readjust to the real world.

What if you could wield the Force?

What if you were related to royalty?

DAD

What Would Happen if...

What if

Chances are, you probably are!

It's good to be a king. Or a queen. Or a prince or princess, duke or duchess, or any true blue-blooded member of any number of royal families holding court across the world today. Royals live in posh palaces staffed by butlers, chauffeurs, stylists, and chefs who cater to their every whim. (Strawberry shortcake for supper? As you wish, Your Highness!) They own private jets and grand palaces. And until not too long ago, kings and queens ruled vast kingdoms with unquestioned authority. But royalty is an exclusive club; unless you raise an army and stake your claim by storming a few castle walls, the only ways to become a member are to marry into the family or by birthright. And while only a very few are lucky enough to be born as a prince or princess, literally everyone you know—yourself included—is actually related to royalty.

TAKE A SEAT

Family Ties

Maybe Dad or Grandma or Aunt Bertha told you about that celebrity in your family history—a Spanish explorer, perhaps, or a Plymouth Rock pilgrim. And while it's cool to claim that a star swung from your family tree, it's actually not that special. Peer far enough back in time and you'd see that *everyone* has someone famous in their family, and this famous family member is related to *everyone* today.

It's simple math. Your two parents had four parents who had eight parents who had 16 parents and on and on until about 1,000 years ago, when every mother and father who lived in, say, Europe, was the common ancestor of everyone alive with European roots today. And, yep, these common ancestors include kings and queens. People are considered *relatives* if they share ancestors, so that means you are related to royalty from as recently as a thousand years ago and quite possibly sooner. "Everyone who has European ancestry today is related to, say,

[ninth-century English king] Charlemagne or William the Conqueror," says geneticist Peter Ralph, who co-authored a paper on the surprising family ties between Europe's past and present. "The same thing is probably true for other similarly sized parts of the Earth, meaning East Asians are related to the Chinese emperors of a thousand years ago, and so on."

Unfortunately, your genetic material from ancient royalty isn't going to get you a guest room at Buckingham Palace or a birthday card from a Saudi prince. Royal families limit their membership through painstakingly recorded lineages that weave through the more complex weblike family histories we share with our common ancestors. But the next time you spot a royal waving on TV, you can wave back and say, "Hey, that's my distant, distant cousin!"

Side Effects Include ...

MUMMY MOMMY

Peel back sufficient layers of history—about 3,500 years' worth—and you will find that everyone living that far back is a common ancestor for *everyone* living today. That means we're all related to the ancient Egyptian king Ramses II and the beautiful Queen Nefertiti. If someone was alive 3,500 years ago, and he or she had children, consider him or her your ancestor. By that same token, you couldn't be a descendant of King Tut, because the famous pharaoh had no living children. But you are a descendant of King Tut's father, Akhenaton.

BUST OF NEFERTITI

PRINCES AND PAUPERS

Your relation with royalty comes with a catch: You're also related to a lot of ancestors who are not royalty. "The amazing thing is," says Ralph, "if you're descended from Charlemagne, then you're descended from *everyone* who was alive at the time who had children—and whose children had children, and so on—so probably about two-thirds of the population. That would mean you're descended from Charlemagne but also the beggars just outside the castle walls."

PORTRAIT OF CHARLEMAGNE

ROYAL PAIN

Just because you're related to royalty doesn't mean everyone must address you as "Your Majesty." Never mind that everyone else is related to royalty right along with you. The truth is, not even real-life siblings of kings and queens had to call their throne-warming kin "Your Majesty," an honorific reserved for European monarchs since the 16th century. The family of England's King George VI nicknamed him "Bertie," short for his first name Albert. So while you don't deserve a fancy title, you can still adopt a fun nickname.

Could it Happen?

Being the descendant of a ninth-century English king or an ancient Egyptian pharaoh is cool and all, but maybe you were hoping for a relation to royalty from more recent history. It's possible. Just ask Sarah Culberson. Actually, make that Princess Sarah Culberson. Adopted just after her first birthday, Culberson grew up as the youngest daughter in a loving family in the suburbs of West Virginia, U.S.A. She became curious about her past in her 20s and began searching for information about her birth parents. What she learned about her father shocked her: He was a ruler of the Mende people in Bumpe, a town in the West African country of Sierra Leone. Culberson was a princess! She traveled to Bumpe to meet her birth father and the people she might one day lead. Hundreds turned out to welcome Princess Culberson home in a ceremony of singing and dancing. But she also found a region torn apart by civil war. Culberson co-founded an organization to help rebuild schools and raise the quality of life for her father's community. Like any good princess, Culberson is helping her people.

PRINCESS SARAH CULBERSON

What if everything was free?

There really is no such thing as a free lunch (or free video console or bike or ...)

Cash, dough, dinero, moolah, scratch, bread, bucks, cabbage—money has so many names for a reason: It plays a big role in our society. Your parents earn it to pay for just about everything you need to survive and live comfortably: food, homes, gas for the family car, electricity, heat, water, Internet, garbage-pickup service, and other important stuff. People invest money in stocks, property, and their education to eventually make more money. We borrow it, save it in the bank, or stash it in a secret place for emergencies. Money doesn't actually make the world go around, but it sure seems that way. What if you suddenly didn't need to spend dough, bread, and cabbage to buy ... well, dough, bread, and cabbage?

Free for All

Movie tickets? On the house! Popcorn with extra butter? Zero bucks! Super-size soda? Free, along with all the refills. In a world where money is literally not an object, an afternoon at the movies wouldn't cost an arm and a leg. You'd no longer need to count the days to your birthday for that new video game console or remote-control drone with the cool Bluetooth camera thing. No summer job? No problem! Just walk into any store and tell the nice salesperson behind the counter that you'll take this, that, and two of those! Why not? Everything is free! Welcome to Easy Street!

Until you hit a dead end. Today our money comes in cash, on plastic credit and debit cards, or in pure electronic form, but it serves the same important purpose as the very first currency, mollusk shells called cowrie, invented by the Chinese more than 3,000 years ago. It's used to trade for goods (food, furniture) or services (house construction, web design) and to assign these things value. People earn money for making useful things (growing food,

building cars) or providing a service (pest control, freelance illustration). In a world where everything was free—without any money—work would have no reward. People wouldn't have any motivation to put in the hours. No one would want to build the bike or design the video game. No salesperson would stand in the store to patiently bag this, that, and two of those for you. Would you?

Before long, everything up for grabs would've been grabbed. Store shelves would sit empty and movie theaters would go dark. With no one motivated to make goods or provide more services, goods and services would go away. You'd be stuck growing your own food and building your own video game system—or figuring out a way to compensate someone else for it. Maybe money can't buy happiness, but it can buy a cheeseburger or that cool Bluetooth drone thing and lots of other stuff that's worth working at an after-school job or saving money from neighborhood chores.

Side Effects Include ...

GRAIN

SEEDS

WANNA TRADE?

In a world without buying, you'll need to barter instead. It's what people did before the invention of money. Tens of thousands of years ago, when humans began establishing villages and farms rather than following herds of animals, they traded for what they needed: animal furs for vegetables, plant seeds for fish, arrowheads for farming tools, grain and candle wax for goats and cows. Then money came along and made the entire process easier. (Bills are easier to cram in your wallet than goats, after all.)

SATISFACTION GUARANTEED

People love getting something for nothing. (Think of how excited you get when you spot a free-sample stand in the grocery store.) But putting in effort makes us happy, too. Researchers call it the "Ikea effect" after the store that sells assemble-it-yourself furniture. "When we make things ourselves—from origami to Ikea furniture—we love them more than if they come preassembled," says Harvard business professor Michael Norton. "When things are too easy to get, like when they're free, we can be sacrificing the pleasure that comes from a job well done."

Could it Happen?

A society without moolah has happened before. The Inca managed to build the largest empire in South America in the 15th century without money of any sort. They didn't even have stores! But that doesn't mean everything was free. Beginning at 15, Inca boys were required to work for the government for up to two-thirds of the year, sweating away on construction projects from palaces to the continent's most extensive network of roads. In return, the workers received all of life's essentials: food, clothes, a place to live—everything except money. A similar labor program was used in ancient Egypt, a kingdom that predated the invention of money.

The Inca didn't have cash, but they still had to work to make a living. Nothing was actually free. A society in which goods and services cost nothing—a true land of the free—is unlikely to form as long as goods and services are scarce, or in limited supply. As long as anything (say, a pizza) costs something (the farmer's cost to grow the wheat for the dough, the trucking company's fuel costs to transport the ingredients, the pizza chef's labor to toss the pizza into the air), nothing will be free.

INCA WINTER SOLSTICE FESTIVAL, CUSCO, PERU

155

24 miles (39 km)

High dive!

If you had stronger balloons, you could continue your ascent to the point where you reach the limits of the atmosphere. In 2012, Austrian skydiver Felix Baumgartner rode a helium balloon 24 miles (39 km) above Roswell, New Mexico, U.S.A. He saluted his capsule's cameras, then stepped into the void, setting the record for the highest skydiving jump.

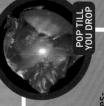

POP TILL YOU DROP

HIGHEST SKYDIVER

37,000 feet (11 km)

Winged winner!

Your balloons carried you high into the sky—but not as high as the highest-flying bird: the Rüppell's vulture, which evolved with a special protein in its blood that lets it soar to the same altitude as a commercial airliner without passing out from lack of oxygen.

RÜPPELL'S VULTURE

32,000 feet (10 km)

Breaking point!

Helium balloons float because the special gas inside weighs less than the surrounding air, displacing—or pushing away—the air as the balloon rises. But a toy balloon has its limits. As the air pressure around the balloon drops, the helium inside expands. Eventually ... pop! Your big bunch of balloons will begin bursting at around 32,000 feet (10 km), before you even leave the Earth's lower atmosphere.

MOUNT EVEREST

30,000 feet (9 km)

Cool ride!

At this height, you could wave hello to mountain climbers summiting Earth's tallest peak: Mount Everest. But this extreme altitude comes with extreme thrills and chills. You've reached the jet stream—a raging river of wind that can reach more than 275 miles an hour (443 km/h). Now you're going places, buffeted along by the same atmospheric currents that commercial pilots use to speed up their flights at this altitude. But pilots and their passengers sit in a cozy pressurized plane. You're exposed to temperatures that drop to nearly minus 100°F (-73°C). Any exposed skin suffers from frostbite, an agonizing condition in which blood drains from fingers and faces to preserve the body's core temperature. Unless you're wearing some kind of space suit to withstand the extreme cold, now might be a good time to let go and parachute to more hospitable altitudes.

26,000 feet (8 km)

Into thin air!

Attention, balloon pilots: Please slip on your oxygen mask. You've drifted into the cheerily named "Death Zone," a region above 26,000 feet (8 km) where the air holds only a third of the oxygen we inhale at sea level. Even with the help of bottled air, you might become a little befuddled and dizzy as oxygen literally leaks from your blood. Just remember to hold tight to those balloons!

OXYGEN MASK

What if

you got caught in a bunch of helium balloons?

You'd better bring a jacket. And an oxygen tank. And a parachute.

The key word here is "big." An ordinary bunch of balloons wouldn't even lift a kitten. A thousand balloons won't budge your soles from the soil. For this silly scenario, you'll need to raid every party-supply store in town, buying enough balloons to fill a two-car garage: about 4,000 of them. Inflated with helium and lashed together like a kaleidoscopic blimp, your big balloon bunch is ready for takeoff. Hold on tight as you reach new heights ...

6,500 feet [2 km]

Bundle up!

You now have your head in the clouds—low level "stratus" clouds, to be exact—and the air is noticeably thinner than it was on the ground. You might begin to feel light-headed if you had to do anything more than just hang out and enjoy the scenery. The drop in temperature, however, is impossible to ignore. Although you're still deep in the troposphere—Earth's lowest level of the atmosphere—the air is already close to freezing. You slip on your hoodie and wrap your free arm around your body, shivering against the cold.

STRATUS CLOUDS

3,000 feet [0.9 km]

Enjoy the view!

The landscape spreads out below you in all directions. Cars look like toys and people look like ants. Soak in the view, because you've passed the height of the world's tallest skyscrapers. The air is slightly thinner at this altitude, but you barely notice. A shiver runs up your spine as the temperature starts to cool.

SKYSCRAPER VIEW

15,000 feet [4.6 km]

Where one man has gone before!

You're not the first person to dream up this loony balloon scheme. In 1982, a truck driver named Lawrence Richard Walters strapped on a parachute, rigged 45 helium-filled weather balloons to a lawn chair, and floated up to 15,000 feet (4.6 km) above Southern California. His plan for landing was simple: Walters began shooting the balloons with a pellet gun until he drifted down to Earth.

LOONY BALLOONER

What if zombies attacked?

Fear not—the government has a plan for that.

They shamble! They stink! They want to munch on your gray matter! Zombies are the nastiest monsters to crawl from pop culture. Half-rotten and smelling like death warmed over, these walking corpses are driven by an insatiable appetite for fresh meat (aka, you). They stumble along with their arms outstretched, clawing after the living, never needing so much as a nap. If one of these creatures sinks its teeth into your tender skin, you'll become a zombie, too. More than just nasty, zombies are infectious! It's a good thing these fiends are fictional. Or are they? Believe it or not, the United States government has a plan in place to deal with an undead uprising. How does this plan pan out?

Drastic Tactics

"Zombie infections have the potential to seriously undermine national security and economic activities that sustain our way of life," begins Section Five, Paragraph A of the Department of Defense's unclassified CONPLAN 8888-11, also known as the "Counter-Zombie-Dominance" plan. Written by defense planners in 2011, this document outlines 31 pages of military operations and guidelines to protect "non-zombie humans" from the threats posed by every type of zombie—including "space zombies" and "vegetarian zombies" (see the zombie varieties opposite). It even covers the rules of engagement with undead enemies, classifying zombies as "pathogenic life-forms" deserving of no special protections from treaties or conventions. In the zombie apocalypse, the military will take no prisoners.

CONPLAN 8888-11's "Zombie-threat summary" describes every kind of undead enemy, including ...

Pathogenic Zombies: Infected deceased that spread their zombie plague by biting and scratching.

Radiation Zombies: Created by an extreme dose of radiation, such as a nuclear bomb.

Evil Magic Zombies: Victims of a voodoo curse or a witch's spell.

Space Zombies: Astronauts exposed to cosmic radiation or extraterrestrial toxins.

Weaponized Zombies: Zombies created deliberately as weapons by mad scientists.

Symbiant-Induced Zombies: Zombies created by parasites, such as the female phorid fly of South America. The fly makes slaves of fire ants by injecting them with her eggs.

Vegetarian Zombies: According to the plan, these zombies are "identified by their aversion to humans, affinity for plants, and their tendency to ... groan the word 'grains.'"

66 "CDRUSSTRATCOM will execute global military operations to protect humankind from zombies and, if directed, eradicate zombie threats to human safety and aid civil authorities in maintaining law and order and restoring basic services during and after a zombie attack." 99

–Mission Statement from the Defense Department's CONPLAN 8888-11, the Counter-Zombie-Dominance plan

See next page for more!

Plan of Counterattack

CONPLAN 8888-11's Zombie-Defying Tips

Like any legit government document, the Pentagon's Counter-Zombie-Dominance plan is dense with jargon and official-sounding orders for various branches of the U.S. military. For instance: "The system of Zombie Conditions (Z-Cons or ZOMBIECONS) will provide predetermined actions to proactively position the USSTRATCOM enterprise in response to threat indications and warnings." But amidst all the unwieldy words and mysterious abbreviations, CONPLAN 8888-11 offers some sensible advice that might actually save your skin in an undead uprising, including ...

Tip 1: Hope for rain. "If civil water supplies are cut off," the plan states, "humans will have to rely on other means to obtain water." Because streams and rivers might be contaminated with zombie germs, your best hope for freshwater will come from the sky. "Rain will be vitally important to human survival," according to the plan.

Tip 2: Steer clear of hospitals. When zombies bite or scratch their victims, those victims usually keel over and become zombies. "Injured humans will likely seek out medical care in hospitals and local clinics," the plan states. "These locations will ultimately become sources of zombieism in and of themselves as victims mutate."

Tip 3: Head for the CDC. Although the plan states "there is no known medical cure for a zombie pathogen," it recommends that survivors seek out the nearest Centers for Disease Control (CDC) for any hope of a medical breakthrough. (And the CDC published a Zombie Preparedness Guide in 2011 as a publicity stunt, so the scientists there have some experience with zombie-apocalypse planning.)

Tip 4: Stock up. According to the plan, "adequate zombie defenses require sandbags, sand, barbed wire, anti-personnel mines, riot-control chemical agents ... and petroleum (to create flame barriers)."

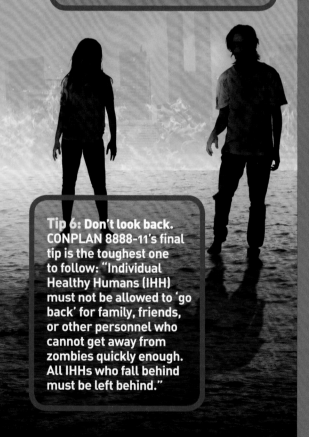

Could it Happen?

Lest you think CONPLAN 8888-11 is some sort of joke from Pentagon officials with too much time on their hands, a disclaimer at the start of the document states "this plan was not actually designed as a joke." But that doesn't mean the U.S. government is preparing for the dawn of the living dead. CONPLAN 8888-11 was created by students at the Pentagon's Joint Combined Warfighting School as an exercise in planning for a real disaster and invasion without naming real-life nations or groups as adversaries—which might lead to political tensions or even real-life conflict. "We elected to use a completely impossible scenario because that could never be mistaken as a real plan," states the disclaimer at the beginning of the document. "The hyperbole involved in writing a 'zombie survival plan' actually provided a very useful and effective training tool. Because the plan was so ridiculous, our students not only enjoyed the lessons, they actually were able to explore the basic concepts of plan and order development very effectively." See? CONPLAN 8888-11 isn't a joke (even if the scenario it describes isn't real).

Meanwhile, the closest thing to a real zombie outside of Hollywood horror movies is from African and Haitian history, which is filled with references to the Z-word. Practitioners of voodoo—a religion that originated in West Africa—believe that sorcerers known as "bokors" could combine spells and "zombie powder" to resurrect the recently deceased and turn them into mindless slaves. The key ingredients of the powder are charred bones, bits of toad, exotic plants, and pufferfish—which contains neurotoxins that can cause paralysis and death. Victims of zombification allegedly expire, then recover in a vegetative state ready to follow orders. Yep, a clear-cut Evil-Magic Zombie as described in CONPLAN 8888-11.

Tip 5: Lotion up. "Marketing materials for most hand sanitizers indicate the product kills 99 percent of all germs," states CONPLAN 8888-11. "It is entirely possible that such products could limit or delay the spread of pathogen-based zombieism."

Tip 6: Don't look back. CONPLAN 8888-11's final tip is the toughest one to follow: "Individual Healthy Humans (IHH) must not be allowed to 'go back' for family, friends, or other personnel who cannot get away from zombies quickly enough. All IHHs who fall behind must be left behind."

What if

Don't go spending all those gold doubloons just yet!

The rule of "Finders keepers, losers weepers" doesn't always apply beyond the playground. Your chances of keeping any fortunes you find depend on the type of "treasure" and where you found it. If that treasure is a misplaced wallet, bag of bills, dropped jewelry, or other lost property worth more than $100, it's your legal obligation in most U.S. states to turn the items over to the police, who will attempt to track down the rightful owners. But what about treasure of the more traditional type: buried or otherwise hidden chests or sacks of gold and silver coins and artifacts? Get ready to strike pay dirt!

Missed Fortune

Depending on where you find your lost "treasure troves," as recovered hoards of gold and silver are called in legal circles, you'll either get to keep the entire hoard or turn it over to the owner of the property (or split the find 50/50 with that owner). Treasure troves are rare in the United States, where gold and silver coins are a relatively new artifact (and despite their portrayals in movies, pirates in U.S. waters usually spent their treasure rather than buried it). In Europe, with its long history of raiders, castles, and kings, such troves are so common that European governments have processes in place and

entire agencies for dealing with them. In England, for instance, all troves more than 300 years old belong to the crown. Treasure seekers must report their findings within two weeks of discovering them. The hunters are rewarded for their efforts, however, and paid a fair value for their treasures (although they must split the cash with the owner of the property on which the treasure was found). The payment encourages treasure hunters to work with the government agency in charge of such treasure troves, which then go on display at a museum for the public to see. In the end, everyone wins.

Could it Happen?

Finding pirate treasure and long-buried artifacts is easy in books and movies. X always marks the spot! But such troves in the real world are never that easy to uncover. The most successful treasure hunters are also amateur archaeologists, piecing together historical records and scraps of maps to pinpoint likely spots for buried hoards. But even armed with local knowledge (and powerful metal detectors), fortune hunters don't strike it rich unless they have one key component: luck. See for yourself in these three tales of lost treasure found ...

Gold Rush

A California couple was walking their dog on their property in 2013 when they spotted something shiny in the dirt. Digging deeper, they unearthed eight cans containing more than 1,400 gold U.S. coins from the mid-1800s.

Value: $10 million

Anglo-Saxon Treasure

An Englishman sweeping a metal detector over a freshly plowed farm field in 2009 hit the jackpot when he discovered enough gold and silver artifacts from seventh-century England to fill nearly 250 bags.

Value: $5.3 million
(split with the farmer who owned the field)

Pirate Plunder

Underwater explorer Barry Clifford discovered the only confirmed pirate shipwreck, off of Cape Cod, Massachusetts, U.S.A., in 1984. The hold of the ship—named the *Whydah*—was crammed with treasure looted from other vessels during the golden age of piracy.

Value: $200 million

BARRY CLIFFORD

What if you could wield the Force?

You'd never need to worry about losing the TV remote again.

Luke Skywalker uses it to blow up the planet-smashing Death Star in the original *Star Wars* film. The courageous Rey wields it to escape from the Starkiller base in *Star Wars: The Force Awakens*. Any force as useful as the Force would be handy to have for saving the galaxy or just livening up friends' birthday parties. You don't even need to be a Jedi Knight to know that. But what if you could transplant that mystical "energy field" from a long time ago in that galaxy far, far away and harness it right here on Earth today? May the Force be with you ...

YODA

Mind Tricks Over Matter

Instead of just a single superpower, the Force of the Star Wars galaxy is more like a Swiss army knife of magical abilities that vary depending on the skill of the wielder. For the sake of this scenario, we'll assume you're a Jedi Knight who hasn't succumbed to the evil "dark side." (That means you can't heat up your burrito with lightning from your fingers. Sorry!) Enhanced strength and agility come with your training (so you'll always have a job as a circus acrobat if you want it), but the real crowd-pleasing Force power is telekinesis. That's the flexing of mental muscles to move objects in the real world—opening doors, lifting heavy objects, and chucking chunks of stuff with just a wave of your hand. Simulate this power by waving your hand in front of automatic doors

JEDI POWER
OF SUGGESTION

or pretending to change the channels on TV with your mind.

A Force wielder's second best party trick is the power of suggestion. In the Star Wars movies, Jedi Knights often get their way just by asking for it in a confident voice and waving their hands to enforce their will on their targets. "These aren't the droids you're looking for," Obi-Wan Kenobi says dismissively to a pair of nosy stormtroopers in the original *Star Wars*. Imagine getting your way just by asking for it! Of course, you would need to use your power only for good—unless you want to fall to the evil dark side and lose all your friends. In fact, you're better off influencing people with your magnetic personality and liberal use of the magic word: please.

Side Effects Include ...

"CLEAR VISION"

TELEPATHY

Think of this power as a cell phone inside your skull: the ability to receive the thoughts and feelings of others and send mental messages in return. Jedi can transmit their thoughts to other Jedi. The catch: They seem better at sending messages after they're dead.

MIND MEETING

CLAIRVOYANCE

A combination of the French words for "clear" and "vision," clairvoyance is the ability to mentally visualize people, objects, or events that are somewhere else—even on the other side of the galaxy! It's like setting up a one-way video feed on your smartphone to anyplace you want.

PRECOGNITION

Perhaps the eeriest of the Force powers, precognition is the ability to foresee the future. Unfortunately, such foresight often takes the form of cryptic images and mysterious visions open to broad interpretation.

SEEING THE FUTURE

Could it Happen?

"The Force is what gives a Jedi his power," explains Jedi Master Obi-Wan Kenobi in the original *Star Wars* movie. "It's an energy field created by all living things. It surrounds us and penetrates us. It binds the galaxy together." The Star Wars prequels added science to the sorcery, linking Force powers to microscopic organisms known as "midi-chlorians" that live within the bodies of Force-wielding Jedis and evil Sith Lords. Regardless of its source, the Force is unfortunately off-limits in our galaxy. But that doesn't mean you can't replicate at least one of its powers! University of Maryland neuroscientist David Poeppel, as part of his research into thought-reading for the U.S. Army, has created a very simple means of synthetic telepathy using a fridge-size medical scanner that measures brain activity. He says we have a long way to go, but "in 50 years, we will be able to transmit at least relatively primitive aspects of thinking, aka telepathy." No word on whether his system will let you pull off any Jedi mind tricks.

What if

you could **control** your **dreams**?

Every night would play out like a superhero movie— with you as the star!

It starts about 90 minutes after your head hits the pillow. Suddenly, you're summiting Mount Everest on a pogo stick. Or you're stumbling into a room of your house you've never seen before. Or you're giving a speech in front of your entire school— except you forgot to put on pants. Don't bother pinching yourself—you're dreaming! What if you could wrestle control of those amazing midnight adventures from your subconscious? Put on your pj's and let's find out!

Pillow Flight

The laws of physics—gravity, the passage of time, the characteristics of light and sound—apply everywhere in the known universe except for one place: dreamland. Once you sink into a state called REM (or rapid eye movement) sleep, your brain takes a vacation from reality and begins creating strange and silly scenarios that engage all five of your senses. If you could take command of your dreamscape, you would suddenly be like a movie director starring in his own film, creating it as you go and giving yourself any roles and powers you could dream of. You might soar! You might travel through time and space! You might relive favorite memories! You might eat a donut the size of Mount Rushmore!

Sweet Dreams

After decades of sleep research, scientists haven't figured out why we dream. They know that all mammals do it, and even some birds and reptiles (some scientists think we inherited the ability to dream from our distant reptile ancestors). But research suggest that dreaming is actually good for you. It may play a crucial role in the forming of memories or coping with painful ones: a way of processing and storing at night everything that happened to you during the day. Dreaming might also make us smarter and more creative during our waking hours. Dreams could even reveal the solution to some problem that you haven't been able to solve while you were awake. So even if you can't take control of your dreams, they're still working for your benefit. If you're feeling drained or stuck, grabbing 40 winks—and a few vivid dreams—might recharge your brain.

Could it Happen?

Sleep experts say we can seize control of our dreams and do all sorts of fantastical things—anything we want, really. But first we need to realize we're actually dreaming *while* we're dreaming. Achieving this deep-sleep state, known as "lucid dreaming," isn't easy. Entire books and websites are devoted to the practice, and wannabe dream masters practice every night for years and still never achieve success. Less than one percent of participants in dream studies manage to enter this crucial dream-controlling state. A variety of masks and headbands promise to help sleepers reach a lucid state by flashing tiny lights above the eyelids during REM sleep. Sleep researchers, meanwhile, have discovered that zapping nappers with a weak electric current for 30 seconds also triggers their lucid dreams—a treatment that might sound like a nightmare. You'll find some less-shocking lucid-dreaming tips below ...

Wake Up Your Mind: How to Seize the Night

Tip 1: Practice when you're awake. Figure out a routine—such as knocking on the wall or reading a particular text file on your smartphone—that you'll repeat a few times every day. If you carry this routine into your dreams and see something weird (your hand might go through the wall, for instance, or the text might appear garbled, which happens frequently in dreams), you'll realize that you're not in the waking world anymore.

Tip 2: Take the lucid-dreaming pledge. Every night, just before you hit the hay and shut down for the day, repeat the following promise out loud three times: "When I dream tonight, I'm going to know it's a dream." You might feel silly saying it, but a nightly reminder will help you get into the lucid-dreaming habit.

Tip 3: Get plenty of sleep. A good night's sleep gives you longer stretches of dream-friendly REM sleep and more opportunities to recognize that you're dreaming. Kids between 5 and 12 need about 11 hours of sleep. Older kids and adults can get by with seven or eight.

Tip 4: Don't freak out. Follow the three tips above and sooner or later you'll achieve a state of lucid dreaming. Your first instinct might be to leap to the moon or spawn a chocolate-spewing volcano, but don't overdo it! Any sudden burst of excitement will wake you up, and you'll be back to reality and its dream-crushing laws of physics. Keep your lucid-dreaming activities simple at first—say, a 30-second hover or a single scoop of strawberry ice cream—before working your way up to lunar leaps and crime-fighting adventures.

Happily Ever After

What if you lived ...

... here?

Mickey maniacs who never want to leave the "happiest place on Earth" in Orlando, Florida, U.S.A., can move into a new neighborhood of nearly 300 houses built right on the grounds of Walt Disney World. The high-end homes pack all sorts of Disney-flavored finishes, such as "hidden Mickey" mouse heads. Residents get year-round access to the theme park in private shuttles. All that Mickey-mousing around comes at a price. The cheapest houses are $2 million.

... down here?

Okay, so you can't really live full-time underwater but you can sleep with the fishes in style for a night at the Atlantis, a hotel in the Middle Eastern nation of the United Arab Emirates. Both the Neptune and Poseidon suites (named, appropriately enough, for ancient water gods) offer posh aquatic accommodations. They feature floor-to-ceiling windows with underwater views of a lagoon teeming with sharks, manta rays, and thousands of other fishy friends. If nothing else, you're guaranteed a deep sleep.

... way up here?

Talk about the high life! After an exhausting day of scrambling up ropes and rock ledges, mountain climbers can crawl into special suspended tents called portaledges and settle in for the night. "They're actually more comfortable than tents on the ground because you don't have any rocks sticking in your back," says adventure photographer Gordon Wiltsie. "You just have to be careful when you cook with the stove. It would be a disaster if the tent burnt up around you!" If you happen to forget where you are in your sleep and tumble out the exit, you won't fall far. "You sleep in your harness and never untie it," Wiltsie says. "That's a basic rule of climbing."

... way down here?

For $800 a night, you can rent the "largest, deepest, darkest, oldest, quietest" hotel room in the world, 220 feet (67 m) below the surface of the Earth at the Grand Canyon Caverns in Arizona, U.S.A. Guests ride an elevator 22 stories down to a room as spacious as, well, a cave: 200 feet (61 m) wide, 400 feet (122 m) long, with a ceiling so high it disappears into the complete darkness of the cave system. It's not an icky cave, either. Because the limestone rock sucks all the moisture out of the air, nothing lives in the cave—not even a bat, rat, or bug.

... way out here?

Moving from place to place—packing and unpacking your stuff, having to make new pals—can be a pain. But what if your house and friends always moved with you? That's the idea behind cruise-ship living, a trend among retirees who book back-to-back cruise vacations rather than spend their sunset years landlocked in a retirement home. It makes sense when you think about it. Cruise ships have all-you-can-eat buffets, medical care, unlimited entertainment options, and exotic ports of call. Guests don't even need to clean their cabins! A cruise ship called The World is actually owned by its passengers, some of whom live full time in 165 private residences ranging from small cabins (costing as much as $600,000) to three-bedroom apartments. Like any cruise ship, The World packs fancy restaurants (four of them!) and lots of luxuries. Residents can vote on where the ship goes next, so that every voyage can bring a new adventure.

169

Index

Boldface indicates illustrations.

Index

Credits